D1138476

The Good Girl's Guide To Being

~~Nicer~~

~~Calmer~~

~~More Patient~~

A D*ck

The Good Girl's Guide To Being

~~Nicer~~

~~Calmer~~

~~More Patient~~

A D*ck

The art of saying what you want,

asking for what you need

and getting the life you deserve

Alexandra Reinwarth

LAGOM

BOOKS FOR A BETTER BALANCED LIFE

Published by Lagom
An imprint of Bonnier Books UK
2.25, The Plaza,
535 Kings Road,
Chelsea Harbour,
London, SW10 0SZ

www.bonnierbooks.co.uk

Paperback – 978-1-788-700-81-8
Ebook – 978-1-788-700-80-1

A CIP catalogue of this book is available from the British Library.

Typeset by EnvyDesign Ltd
Printed and bound in Great Britain by Clays Ltd, Elcograf S.p.A.

3 5 7 9 10 8 6 4 2

Copyright © Alexandra Reinwarth, 2018
First published in Germany by mvg Verlag, 2016
First published by Blink Publishing in 2018
Translated by Annette Charpentier

Alexandra Reinwarth has asserted her moral right to be identified
as the author of this Work in accordance with the Copyright, Designs
and Patents Act 1988.

Contents

Introduction

It all began when I said 'Fuck you!' to Catherine. I should mention that I normally don't say things like that to people. Generally, I'm not that generous with invitations to have sex, not under any circumstances.

But Catherine, it so happens, is one of those people who forever gives you the feeling that you have just made a big mistake and that you now owe them. Do you know people like that? People who are always complaining but never change anything? People who suck out your life energy like young children suck Ribena out of its carton with a straw?

Catherine loves dwelling in a valley of tears. If you took her at face value you would think she was depressed. But during our relationship I came to realise that she is not at all depressed – she is just a very silly cow.

Life seemed to permanently deal a bad hand to Catherine: her job was lousy, her relationship with her boyfriend was on the brink, her family habitually blamed her for everything, her future was bleak, and she was at a complete loss in terms of what to do. But while I was busy worrying about her, Catherine went on a cruise, had lots of parties and married her boyfriend.

One time, I felt so sorry for her (*'My marriage is practically over'*) that I suggested that she go on a city break to Venice with her husband. It was totally my idea for the two of them to do something nice together. I looked after their dog, watered their plants and topped up their seawater pool with salt. Catherine's house is not exactly around the corner from mine. Also, her house is very big, modern and extremely expensively kitted out – despite the huge financial commitments she is burdened with.

Catherine, so she claims, is far too good for this world. She once had building work done and paid the workmen on time. Then she boasted how virtuous she was that she didn't make them wait for the money for three months or fob them off with half the sum.

'I thought of the man's family,' she said with tears in her eyes, looking like a saint.

When we met up after the Venice trip she was in a bit of a hurry – she urgently had to take her husband to his massage, because the beds, in the hotel I had recommended, were a *cat-as-tro-phe*. The whole trip had been a disaster, but she had coped as usual and put on a brave face.

When we next met up, her mother was ill, which she told me about in a voice that one could only assume meant her mum would pop her clogs the very next day. In short, there is always something going wrong for Catherine. Everything is a heavy burden – nothing less. As it happened, Mum just had a headache or an ingrown toenail or whatever.

Do you get the gist? It was always the same – Catherine was all about Catherine. At some point, I realised I didn't like orbiting Catherine's world like a satellite any more – because I am a person, too.

I have no idea why I didn't send Catherine packing a long time ago, even though my partner, L., had suggested that I do so time and again. At first, I wasn't aware of the fact that she was using me, and I also simply tried to avoid confrontations. But during an overhaul of my life while I undertook my Happiness Project,[1] I came to the conclusion: I need to get rid of Catherine. I need to become a bit of a dick.

Until then, I had never finished a friendship with a female friend. Ever. The normal course of things is that the two of you don't get on so well any more, you meet up less and less often, and then the whole thing quietly disappears. Done, no one is harmed, these things happen.

---

1 *Das Glücksprojekt*, mvg Verlag, ISBN-13:978-3868822052

But the kind of friends who suck you dry like a leech, you simply can't get rid of easily. I wasn't quite sure how I could manage this 'letting go' of a friend. How could I behave firmly, without wriggling like a worm on a hook? I found the mere idea of it so *awkward*.

L. made a very pragmatic suggestion: 'You just go to her and say: "Catherine, you're doing my head in and I don't want to see you any more."' Then he stopped, thought about it and added: 'You stupid cow.' L. never liked Catherine.

I know there are people who would do exactly that. But not me. On the contrary, I play for the team that forever apologises when someone pushes them.

To avoid the whole thing, I thought of different strategies:

- I would send L. to say it.
- I would take on a new identity and pretend to Catherine that, sadly, I had died.
- Sadly, actually die.

When the big moment came, and Catherine and I were sitting face to face in a café, she luckily behaved so impossibly that I could utilise the huge surge of anger inside me and surf on it towards the very moment I said:

'Catherine?'

'Yes?'

'Fuck you!'

For lots of people, this would not have been a big thing,

but I felt like a six-foot-six Joan of Arc. Leaving the café, I felt like I was walking in slow motion and, like boxers on their way to the ring, my exit was accompanied by a rousing tune, trumpets and all. I threw my scarf with such verve around my shoulders that I set a stack of innocent menu sheets from the nearby counter flying. As they gently sailed towards the floor, I left the place with my head held high. I wouldn't have been amazed if a faithful horse had been waiting for me outside to take me to more dangerous adventures.

'Hey! Joan of Arc wasn't a boxer ...' L. interrupts my story later that evening and looks at me quite confused. Men sometimes don't listen properly, do they? I imagine that they hear some quiet background rustling, take in two or three significant phrases and make up the rest in their heads. If those words don't make sense together, they have a problem.

Of course, I'm not particularly interested in French national heroines or even boxing; it is not even about Catherine and her stupid salt-water pool. It is about the fact that these two little words – 'fuck you!' – can put you in such a sky-high mood.

'I think it is about freedom,' said Anne, my esoteric friend, when I told her about my moment of pride, and I think she is right. It was a liberating act, but the whole imagery of music and trumpets and a horse wasn't caused by the fact that I had liberated myself from Catherine, the silly cow, but because in a single moment I had liberated myself from my own petty, self-imposed, restricting rules. To simply do what seemed right for me – without a single consideration about whether the other person still liked me afterwards. Wonderful! Shouldn't we always behave like that? Be open and direct? But where exactly is the line between being honest and being a complete dick?

In the following weeks, I noticed many other situations where my behaviour was triggered by what other people would think of me and not by what I wanted to actually achieve myself. (I didn't just notice that my life without Catherine was much better. Which it was.) Why did I put make-up on in the morning when all I was doing was taking our son to playgroup? Hell, no! *Why did I do that?* The depressing answer is that I wanted to make a good impression on the other parents. But I don't really like 90 per cent of them. On the subject of 'liking': why did I go to the office Christmas party? Because I like my boss and my colleagues? Nope! And why am I still in this stupid WhatsApp group that's responsible for my mobile vibrating all through the night like other people's sex toys? The more I thought about it, the more I realised: I spent far too much time with people I didn't like, in places I didn't want to be, doing things I didn't want to do.

How terrible is that?

The more issues I could think of, the more detailed my

plan for freedom became. If merely banishing Catherine from my life had been such an amazing success, what kind of wonderful life was ahead of me when I cancelled all the other things that didn't agree with me at all?

If, for example, I said to my colleagues in the office: 'Thank you, but I don't want to come for a drink after work. No, not just today, but generally', that would be so much better than my usual strategy of inventing absurd excuses and then tripping myself up trying to remember the lies. For example:

'Is your sister better?'

'Sorry? I don't have a sister!'

That has really happened.

'Do you see what I mean?' I asked L. the same evening, when he was chopping up vegetables.

'Hmm, well, yes,' he mumbled. 'It's only ... I hope it's not a plan to turn into a selfish git ...'

'Oh no!' I protested, but, of course, he was right. There was quite a considerable chance that during this liberating campaign of mine I would turn into a dick, but I felt like I would be able to deal with that. I was full of energy – my life would be wonderful! If I only invested my time, my energy (and my money) in things, people and situations that would make me happy – well, that would be amazing, wouldn't it?

'Wouldn't it?' I asked my little boy, who was enthusiastically clinging to my legs.

'Chocolate,' he said, as usual, because it is his favourite word.

Exactly. Chocolate.

If you believe your life could do with a bit more freedom, leisure, self-determination and chocolate, and fewer Catherines, WhatsApp groups and Christmas parties – you are in the right place. We will investigate the following:

- How not to give a damn about other people or issues.
- How not to mutate into a dick at the same time.
- What criteria are helpful to distinguish between what is really important and what is not.
- How small decisions can have a huge impact on the quality of your life.

We will also try quite a funny little exercise about how not to give a toss any more. And I will point out a few hurdles I stumbled over in the course of sorting all this out.

Before we start, here is the promised funny exercise. It is a visualisation, by which I mean an image that we create in our head and can recall at any point. I hope you like it as much as I do.

Right, let's try it. You know bullfighters, don't you? The ones who say 'Olé!', those toreros with firm buttocks and silly clothes? Imagine you are a bullfighter. And now imagine you had one of those red capes they use to attract the bulls. Got it? Good.

No matter what we are going to encounter in this book and in life – everything that you are determined not to give a toss about any more – just visualise letting it gallop towards you, getting faster and faster and then, just before it reaches you, imagine yourself taking an elegant side-step like a bullfighter and letting it run past you at full speed. *Olé*!

There is another Ole who will help you through the following pages. When I was still pondering how amazing it would be to only do what is important to me, I remembered someone who has always done exactly that (as well as my son, who is very good at it): my friend Ole.

Ole is a childhood friend and a very successful business-man. He appears to be seven foot tall, he's a lovely guy AND he never does anything that he doesn't want to do. Needless to say, Ole isn't in any WhatsApp group and only attends the office Christmas party if he knows he will enjoy himself. Despite this, he is popular as a boss, he has many friends and a wonderful family.

He is not the guy, though, who would help you move house, and he would not enthusiastically clap when you recite your favourite poetry, even if you asked him really nicely. But that's all right, that's just the way he is. And everybody likes him.

When someone at work asks me to quickly go over a

The Good Girl's Guide To Being A D*ck

document, I tend to say, 'Sure, pass it over.' That is the exact reason I always run out of time with my own work, get stressed and end up angry with myself.

When someone asks Ole whether he could quickly check this or that, he says: 'Nope.' And he won't do it. Consequently, he has more time, is less stressed, he doesn't get mad at himself and still everybody likes him, because he is a lovely bloke.

On my journey to not giving a toss any more, Ole has helped me a lot simply by imagining how he would react in a tricky situation. It is like Ole is standing right next to me – all seven feet of him – saying: 'You will not do this under any circumstances, my dear.'

Do you know someone like him? If so, imagine him or her standing right next to you. But if you don't know anyone like Ole, I will lend you mine.

So, let's start.

Why it is so difficult not to care

Let's explore why it is so difficult to say to our friend Tom in a nice and normal manner: 'Dear Tom, I wish you all the best for your poetry slam tonight in Overton-on-Stickleback, but I won't be coming. I urgently have to ... lie on the sofa at home with my husband and the dog.'

For some people, the mere idea of saying something like that can be so *awkward* that instead of cuddling on the sofa with their chosen one, they would rather sit on a wobbly chair in the town hall of Overton-on-Stickleback, sipping a warm white wine and listening to poems that go like:

> *Bell, bell, what's this hell*
> *Taste, taste, what's the haste*
> *Bear, bear, what's to bear*
> *Honk, honk, he comes near*
> *Tackle, tackle, we will flee*
> *Flee flee, to the sea ...!*

This is not an exaggeration.

And then you drive home, bark at your partner and the dog because they had such a cosy evening, and go to bed sulking. Sometimes you find yourself already attempting to come up with an excuse for next Wednesday, because Tom has another gig in Underton-on-Stickleback.

That cannot be right.

You don't have to listen to Tom's poems just because you like him. You don't suddenly have to *not* give a damn about Tom himself. But you are allowed to skip the poetry events from now on.[2]

It isn't really surprising how easily embarrassed we all are. From day one we are trained to be nice, not to embarrass others and to be considerate. Don't get me

---

2 Just a few words about poetry events in general: they are brillant. Really. The poems sometimes are very funny, clever, moving and fantastic. Sadly, Tom's are none of these things.

wrong, that's a good thing. I think it is great when people are trained from day one not to behave like arseholes – even though, God knows, it doesn't always work. At the same time, I would appreciate it if we also had the option of finding things, people or situations downright stupid. Here is a very recent example from the nursery down the road.

There is an old German nursery rhyme about a dancing cat: a cat is dancing on her own, and then various animals come and ask her to dance with them. But the cat finds fault with every single one: the rabbit is too wobbly, the dog barks too loudly, the hedgehog is too prickly, etc., until in the end the tomcat turns up and he 'strokes her fur and kisses her gently, and all of a sudden, she dances with him'.

It is a wonderful song, promise. In my opinion, anyway. But it seems it is not politically correct any more. So that none of the children who are acting out the dance-loving animals get rejected, the whole song is now reworded in such a way that every animal gets a chance to dance with the cat. Each animal whispers something in the cat's ear, and each time she complies. Why, oh why? Why can't the cat find the hedgehog far too prickly to dance with? He *is* prickly.

In my opinion, one should not have to dance with partners who are wobbly, loud, awkward or prickly at all. Nope.

And even when the cat finds her tom, the story doesn't

end there any more. Instead the tomcat brings all the others into the circle, and they all dance together, with a jump here, and a jump there, until the sun goes down, and they all go home.

Everybody must do everything together. It's like being in a group of tourists, all marching behind someone ahead, holding a flag. There is no escape. Once you are grown up, you will bear the consequences of this brainwashing shit and you will find yourself sitting on the wobbly chair in the town hall of Overton-under-or-over-Stickleback.

Taking it even further, children are also encouraged to give up their toys to other random children, a tendency spreading now through playgrounds all over the country. It's madness: Leon has a car, but then Ben wants it too. Could be tricky. And immediately Leon's mother comes running and delivers her lecture to the little boy: 'Now then, give little Ben your car, you have played with it for quite a long time, and Ben would be *sooo* happy ...' She goes on and on until a grumpy Leon, close to tears, passes on the car. But it is *his* fucking car! Tough for little Ben. During the next stage of his life, it will take quite a few Kevins and Damians from the nearby problem neighbourhood to undo this.

Children have the ability to not give a crap about unimportant things from the day they are born. Just like dogs. They follow the principle: 'If you cannot play with it or eat it, just piss on it and let it be.'

But children also act by the pleasure principle. They

do not make conscious decisions. The pleasure principle works like this:

Chocolate = good = eat as much as possible

Only later, after quite a few tummy aches, will this principle be questioned.

During puberty, it gets difficult. Other people's opinions are now immensely important. This isn't just about hairstyles or taste in music or clothes; it concerns the whole person. During this phase, when people are extremely insecure and confused, they look for role models and try to emulate the image that seems to be most popular.

Girls find this even more difficult than boys, because the confusing role of being a 'woman' is added to the mix. It's suddenly important what the media in general have to say about everything. My son, not even three years old, expressed this quite succinctly after he had watched some advertising on telly. *'Woman naked, man talks.'* For this reason, for girls, everything revolves around their own appearance – and some people never lose this focus.

Let's start with this topic.

1

You as a Person

- Bikini body
- General looks
- Self-improvement

It makes sense to start with oneself. Everybody has a vague sense of wanting to improve something. My bum should be smaller, my bank balance bigger, my self-esteem more stable, my sex life somehow more exciting, and yes, it might be a good idea to do more exercise. Let's start ... let's start with chocolate.

In normal life, people somehow keep a certain weight without much starving or eating like a horse (Christmas time is an exception). This 'normal' weight has nothing, absolutely nothing to do with the shape one is supposed to have for a so-called bikini body.

The 'bikini body'

A bikini body is what the general public thinks of as a shape fit for a bikini. Last time I had that I was twelve. Ever since then, bikinis and my body have lived on different planets that could never be reunited. At times, there were not even diplomatic relations between them. From the tender age of thirteen – and I can tell you that's quite a few years ago – until very recently, I pulled in my tummy every single summer. Between June and September, on the beach, by the sea and in the swimming pool, I only dared to take very shallow breaths and, in the eighties, when baring your midriff was fashionable, I hardly ever took a breath. It is amazing that I didn't suffer any long-term damage...

Thanks to popular women's magazines, I also knew how to best camouflage my surplus fat. Lying down on a towel or blanket, there was only one possible position: on my back, legs slightly raised – because then they look slimmer. Only those skinny, lanky types of girls confidently sat upright in the lotus position or whatever way they liked sitting ... but they always kept their T-shirts on to distract from their non-existent breasts. See, there is always something.

My behaviour nowadays is more relaxed. But not totally. I still catch myself sitting on the edge of a chair, because that makes my thighs look slimmer. I must have trained myself to do this at some stage. Behaviour like this happens automatically, like when people with bad teeth automatically smile with their mouth closed. I know that in this life the perfect 'beach body' is not achievable for me. But I still feel an urge to work towards it. Like a solemn reminder, I own a pair of jeans one size smaller than I normally take, and if they could, the jeans would raise an eyebrow every time I stand in front of the wardrobe in my underpants.

The most absurd aspect of this story is that in real life I find women particularly attractive when they appear to be confident and self-assured with their big nose, their frizzy hair, their wide hips and their ample tummy.

Maybe this 'woman naked/man talking' thing that my son spotted is the real culprit, but I think it is about time to ask yourself:

Do I have a bikini body or at least something approaching one?

'A bikini body means that someone who has a body is wearing a bikini, nothing more,' I explain to Anne, who is sitting in the car with me. We are on our way to the lake to go swimming.

I will test out some new resolutions, so, for research purposes, I have taken a day off to go swimming with Anne. I explain to her my new determination not to give a damn about my figure when wearing a bikini. 'Hey!' I protest, because as soon as I tell her this she gives my behind an ever-so-brief glance.

We arrive, put our towels down on the grass, and when

Do I have a bikini body, or something close to it?

☐ Yes   ☐ No, not really

Am I prepared to eat less for the forseeable future,
and do lots of exercise? Honestly?

☐ Yes   ☐ Erm ... no

Do I think only skinny women are pretty?

☐ Yes   ☐ Nope

Skip this chapter   WTF!

Anne pulls her flimsy dress over her head, I immediately am incredibly envious of her long and slender legs, her flat tummy and her hip line, where no doughnut has ever docked. Anne is a vegan and only eats organic food. She goes without white sugar, white flour, lactose and frozen food, not to mention the phase when she tried to live on only light. We still take the piss about that.

In my next life I will have legs like that, and I will wear miniskirts, super-tight skinny jeans and hot pants.

'And in my next life, I will have a cleavage,' Anne sighs. We have both brought a bikini, and I have barely jumped into mine and stood up in my full splendour when I automatically pull my tummy in. If I could pull in my backside, my thighs and my hips, I would do that too.

I exhale consciously, relax, and my belly slips into its normal place.

'Just lie down like when you go to sleep, that's probably the most comfortable position,' Anne suggests, and it sounds all right.

'Well? How does it feel?' she asks after a few moments, while I am lying stiffly on my side.

'You know those pictures of beached whales?' I reply, and that is a very apt image. I don't feel good. Not lying on my side, not sitting up and definitely not sitting cross-legged. I am acutely aware of my various wrinkles and surplus fat jostling between me and my real shape, and it is making me miserable.

'Why do I find it so difficult to do without sugar, fat and other such stuff? Or to resist a second pudding? Why can't I get my buttocks to take part in one of those exercise from hell programmes? Or, damn it, why can't I wrap up the chocolate bar and put it away after having eaten one little piece?' I wail.

'Because you love chocolate,' someone says behind me.

It is L., with his beach towel, the dog and our son. L. has taken some time off and even brought us a giant watermelon.

There they are, grinning at me – and then, all of a sudden, there is no room for grumpiness any more. I carry my son in his shark-patterned swimming trunks to the water. The dog is watching us, wagging his tail, and L. cuts the melon into slices. There is a fleeting thought, while my son and I are playing sea-monsters, that my figure is not at its most advantageous like that, but then we squeal with laughter, and I forget it.

During the race back to the others I also forget that I probably don't look like a gazelle, simply because I am laughing. I briefly wince when I sit down cross-legged to eat the melon, but as soon as I look at my loved ones, I feel happy and secure. It is strange. When I distract myself with a good feeling, of friendship, love, goodwill and laughter, there is no room for negative thoughts.

Some brief glances to the left and right are also helpful, because you won't be lying between Jennifer Lopez and Chris Hemsworth. I stop looking down at myself, but rather at the melon juice spreading over my son's face. I look at L.'s bright eyes and listen to Anne's funny story about her last shamanic retreat.

As the sun gets more and more golden, I move closer to L., and together we watch Anne and our child throwing stones into the lake.

'Would you sometimes rather be slimmer, taller, more muscular or somehow different?' I ask L.

He looks at me askance.

'Would *you* rather I was slimmer, taller, more muscular or somehow different?' he replies.

I give him a quick scan from top to bottom, and no, I would not want him any other way. I want him exactly how he is.

'Then I don't want to be different either', says L.

When our son is sound asleep in his cot that evening and I am scoffing a second pudding (pannacotta with morello cherries), I'm not only happy about the lovely day we had, but I have also got an all-round tan, and not only on my tummy. And that is the reason why a pair of jeans, one size too small, land in a recycling bag the next day with a loud *Olé*! Maybe they will end up with Catherine and a few women's magazines, and they can all complain amongst themselves.

Not giving a crap about your looks in general

Looks are a tricky issue. I remember a lightbulb moment when, as a teenager, I went shopping with my mother. All of a sudden, she stopped and looked at me completely flabbergasted – she had realised that on this lovely afternoon in this busy shopping centre men were no longer looking at her but at me! *Wham*! It was as if someone had pulled a switch.

That day I assumed she was annoyed about it, but it was the opposite. When the surprise subsided, she was delighted.

'It is as if a burden has fallen from my shoulders,' she said, grinning.

As a teenager I could not understand this. What was liberating about not getting attention any more? After all, that was the central point in one's life around which everything else revolved. If ever I become as old as her, I thought, science will have invented something that can stop me from looking old!

After a long and contemplative look in the mirror I can assure you that science hasn't achieved this. But now I can understand why my mother seemed so delighted that day. The burden she was shedding in the shopping centre was one she had taken on herself. She too had tried to conform to an image of herself as a good-looking woman. That is hard work. And with time it gets even harder. Only when it seemed in vain could she let go of it and lean back, relaxed, thinking, 'I've finally left all that behind.'

I haven't left it behind yet, but the idea to lean back instead, to stop using all sorts of aids and devices in an attempt to look radiant on a Monday morning, is simply too tempting.

We attend to our looks for other people. Always. When

we claim that we would do all that stuff with eyeliner-mascara-concealer-powder just for ourselves, it is maybe due to the fact that in battle dress, with our armour on, we feel stronger when it comes to meeting the eyes of the world. That, no doubt, is a lovely feeling, but it ultimately stems from the fact that we care about the judgement of the person in the bakery, in the cafeteria, the other parents in the nursery and the check-out bloke in the supermarket. We are admitting that their opinions regarding our looks matter. Not our politeness, reliability, spending power or table manners.

If you want, you can dress and make yourself up to the hilt every morning. But whoever answers 'Absolutely not!' to the question, 'Do you care about what Mr Brown in the office or Ben's dad think about your eyelashes?' can really do without the elaborate paintwork every day. You could have another cup of coffee or a longer hot shower instead, without nicking your legs while shaving them in a hurry and causing a blood bath on the bathroom carpet. You could even play another round of *Candy Crush* on the sofa! Doesn't that sound wonderful?

The next Sunday, when I step outside our house without make-up, in jogging bottoms and an oversized T-shirt, the rubbish bag in one hand, I feel like Britney Spears in her wildest times. Only the paparazzi hiding in a tree are missing. To set myself apart from the winos in front of the supermarket down the road, already emptying

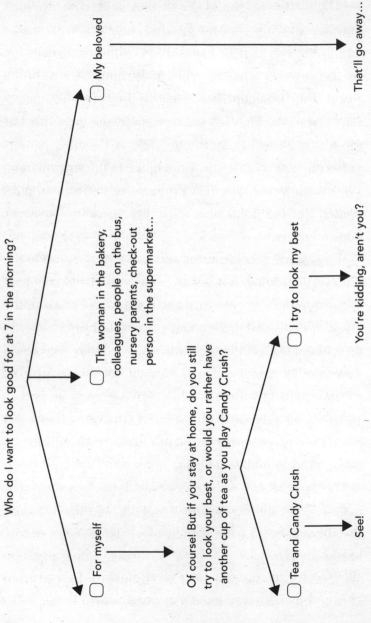

Who do I want to look good for at 7 in the morning?

My beloved

That'll go away...

The woman in the bakery, colleagues, people on the bus, nursery parents, check-out person in the supermarket...

I try to look my best

You're kidding, aren't you?

For myself

Of course! But if you stay at home, do you still try to look your best, or would you rather have another cup of tea as you play Candy Crush?

Tea and Candy Crush

See!

mega bottles of cider, I have added a nice scarf to my outfit.

Even before I get to the bakery, I have gained a new insight. Quite contrary to my expectation, I don't feel at all insecure, uneasy or anything else starting with in- or un-. Quite the opposite: I am this fantastically relaxed, confident, poised woman who doesn't need mascara because of her sheer personality and charm. I don't need make-up! Look at me! I feel seven foot tall, simply because I haven't made an effort! Before I start walking around the bakery waving to people with a bent arm like the Queen, it's my turn to be served, and for the first time my mood is better than one of the baker's salespeople.

In fact, my mood is brilliant. At home they still recognise me, but I think I am ready for the next level: I'll go to work without make-up. I work at home quite often, but also frequently in the office. It is an advertising agency. I don't know whether you are familiar with that kind of environment but everything is ultra-chic and as cool as possible. There are coffee machines costing as much as a small car (and are nearly as powerful); there are little towels smelling of lemongrass in the toilet; there are fruit bowls everywhere as well as tiny chocolate bars. It is wonderful – everything glitters and shines with chrome and glass. But the saying 'it's what's on the inside that counts' doesn't exist here. This doesn't apply to the staff, of course, but they do try to adapt to their environment. Everybody is chic and modern and as cool as possible. No matter what the country's hipsters wear or carry or drag, the horn-rimmed glasses, the full beards, the undercut and those stupid long knitted hats dropping between the shoulder blades – everything that makes you wonder 'Is that meant to look like that?' – you can be sure it has its origin in an advertising agency.

And it is this very place I intend to enter 'naked'. You might think that would be just right, as the 'nude look' is in fashion at the moment: the 'natural look' is mega-in.

'The nutter's look?' asks L. the night before. He finds it hilarious.

'Ha ha,' I reply and pinch him.

'But seriously, it's perfect, this *nude look*. Your new experiment won't be noticed at all – and I can use the bathroom a bit earlier ...' he sniggers. But only an amateur would think that *nude* would have anything to do with going without make-up. For the clueless: to look like you are not wearing any make-up, you first need foundation which is applied with a make-up brush – from the nose towards the side of the face, while carefully leaving the hairline free. Then a transparent matte powder is applied in circular movements with a larger brush over the whole face. The natural shape of the eyebrows is enhanced with a slanted brush and brow powder, or a matte eyeshadow, followed by a finishing fixing gel. After applying the eyeshadow base, one dabs on a shadow in light beige over the whole lid, but the fold is accented with a darker shade of brown. Then you draw a fine line in dark brown eyeliner just above the upper lashes. With the same colour you accent the lower lashes, but you should only use a brush and an eyeshadow pad. Then you treat the upper and lower lashes with an enhancing mascara, apply some concealer (a shade lighter than the foundation) under the eyes, dab a preferably natural-looking rouge on the cheek bones and, to complete the natural look, put on some lip gloss or lipstick.

L. looks at me, suitably aghast. 'You made that up,' he says hopefully, but no, it is the bitter truth. I, however, will interpret the nude look in a totally new way and simply not wear any make-up whatsoever; only the jogging bottoms will be replaced by a pair of jeans.

'You have to do it properly,' L. says the next morning when, before I leave the house, I look in the hall mirror twice. We had a lovely and relaxed morning, I had a good breakfast, our son was happy. I have done some stretches at the open window, hummed while getting dressed and even managed two rounds of *Candy Crush*. A top morning, compared with a 'normal' morning when I spend most of my time in the bathroom, create chaos in my wardrobe and then quickly down some coffee like I'm pouring water on a bushfire.

L., muesli bowl in hand, accompanies me to the door. 'Maybe you should really ignore how you look and not use the mirror last thing before you go.'

Damn it! L. is right. Instead of having no thoughts at all about my looks I had another image in mind: I was a celebrity in Los Angeles on my way to fitness training, the type that still gets recognised despite the big shades and the hair pulled up in a pony tail, with one or two strands decoratively loosened. My looks were still important. I had just found a different image to emulate.

OK, I will leave without getting acknowledgement from the hall mirror.

'But you would tell me if I had something stuck between my teeth or if my hair was completely frizzy?'

'Of course,' L. answers, grinning. How I hate it when I don't know whether he is lying or not!

On my way to the office I need to be careful not to look into the reflecting windows of parked cars to check whether visually all is well and in the green zone. It is mad how automatically and often one tries to look at one's image. Contrary to yesterday, today I don't feel at all like waving at people with a bent arm like the Queen. Quite the opposite – I duck. Up the stairs, along the corridor, into the office. What a stupid idea it is that all the walls in this office are made of glass!

'Hi,' I greet my workmate, Eva, hoping that she won't notice my appearance.

'What has happened to you?' is the response, dashing that hope immediately.

'What? Is it a law here to always look like you're straight

out of a magazine?' I bark at her and demonstratively pull up my slightly too wide but who-the-hell-cares jeans.

'Oh, no,' she replies with a smile – in my opinion, a bit too smiley. Is she grinning?

'What is it? Do I look really bad? Tell me!' I beg her as I outline my new experiment, explaining that I am trying not to care about my looks any more.

'Well, how bad is it?' I repeat my question, and she says: 'Honestly?'

'Yes!' I nod several times.

'To be honest, you have never looked so bad,' Eva says conclusively. 'Not even after the Christmas party in 2012, and that's saying something.'

Within three seconds I am in the ladies and, sadly, I have to agree with her.

'Well, well,' I nod to my mirror image. This really is extraordinary. For starters, my jeans are hanging halfway down, and not in the relaxed style of boyfriend jeans, but in a pathetic down-at-heel kind of way. That says it all. The image is enhanced by the antennae-like frizz on top of my head. I could strangle L.

'Beep, beep, beep!' Eva, who has followed me to the loo, is laughing and fingering my hairdo. 'Come on, let's get you sorted,' she says and removes some chocolate spread leftovers from my son's goodbye kiss on my cheek with a wet wipe.

While lovely Eva is helping me as best she can, I start

thinking: why is my outfit completely normal at the baker's, but not in the office? Why am I embarrassed in this environment dressed like that? It's not only the chocolate spread on my face. Is what my colleagues think of me more important than how the lovely woman in the baker's shop sees me? Am I not embarrassed in front of her delicious loaves? Do I feel less competent in this outfit?

No, it isn't that. It is something completely different. Everybody here makes an effort to look smart and decent. That is an unwritten rule. It's like going to the opera. In terms of the singing, the staging and the production, it is completely irrelevant whether you turn up to watch in an evening dress or in jeans. The audience could practically wear anything, including overalls and shorts; the production would be exactly the same. Why, then, does everybody turn up looking their best? Suits, hair gel, dresses, nice shoes, jewellery and little clutch bags. It is simply part of it. Not in regard to the opera itself, but to the experience of going to the opera. All this, together with the sparkling wine in the interval, the chandeliers and the sea of red velvet, creates a certain kind of magical holiness that makes us *enter* an opera house and not shuffle in. Wearing everyday clothes would be taking something away from the people who have made the effort, who have taken the time and trouble to get their elaborate hairdo done beforehand. It would be like exposing their ambitions. And that wouldn't be very nice.

My office is not an opera house, but it is a kind of stage, and the people who work here create the show day after day. If I turn up there in my slum look, I am the spoilsport, the Grinch. Although it's good that I don't give a damn about my looks, maybe I should care about the unspoken rules?

Next week I'm going to a class reunion – I will try and look good, so good that my failed love interest from those days will be stunned. Ha!

My lovely relaxed mornings can be saved, despite some compromises, but that has cost me seventy-five quid in the form of these purchases:

- Some super moisturising lotion
- The best long-wear eye pencil

My two new friends were not cheap, but they can create magic. In less than five minutes I can look great – if I want to. And sometimes I do want to.

Self-improvement? Screw that!

Once you have accepted that in this life you won't have the ideal beach body, you can also accept a few other things straight away. For example, not only will I never get rid of my little tummy in this life, but also, I won't ever become a tidy person. Furthermore, I won't ever manage to hand in my tax return on time or buy Christmas presents nice and early, and it also looks like I won't give up a cigarette or two during my late, alcoholic nights out with Jana. YES, I KNOW, IT DAMAGES MY HEALTH!

There has always been a depressingly long list of habits and characteristics of mine that I wanted to change. To L.'s annoyance, this list also included some characteristics and habits of his. Only the dog and the child were excluded from my determination to improve – the dog for reasons of being stubborn and unteachable, and our son because he will see it as unloving discipline and, for me, that is simply a no-no!

I have always been absolutely sure that sometime in the future, if I only made enough of an effort, I would be exactly like I wanted to be. I would attend my yoga and Pilates classes regularly, buy all the vegetables in the market, and the shelves in the living room would not look as if someone had simply thrown a ton of books at them from a three-metre distance. In the run-up to Christmas, I would be in an excellent mood; I would sing carols with my son and make a Christmas cake; I would check Pinterest for how to decorate presents with painted pinecones I collected on a walk in the snowy woods. At some point, my life will be like that. That will be about the same point in time when L. and I will spend so-called quality time together in the evenings, and he will whisper some crazily romantic things in my ear, and I will giggle with embarrassment. 'You bastard, we're in a restaurant, everyone can hear us!' This is how it will be. That is my real life. And until then, I simply muddle through. I am like the very hungry caterpillar: at some point I will turn into a beautiful butterfly, but right now I will quickly eat another piece of cake, an apple, and a cheese sandwich ...

This is the classic trap of 'When ... then'. *When I finally am/have something, then this will happen!* You always see this person you could be with your inner eye – if only you made enough of an effort. But somehow you don't quite manage it, even though society, women's magazines and self-help books are in a constant loop of telling you: *If you only work hard enough, you can achieve **everything!***

But this is not true. Look around. We are all caterpillars. And during this caterpillar stage we feel permanently guilty: we've just wasted another afternoon surfing the net, just had another million-calorie sandwich, we've done no sit-ups today and the pinecones ... well ...

Maybe I can order them online. And then, another year is over, and taking stock of the past twelve months, well, we caterpillars might just as well get absolutely hammered. Anybody got a ciggy?

It is a dilemma. But I have also experienced the feeling – when I really got it together and achieved my ideal, just on a small scale – that it didn't work. I would cycle, with a pretty wicker basket on the handlebars, to the weekly market. But generally it would start to rain, the dog's leash would get entangled in the wheels, the fucking wicker basket would tip over and all the lovely healthy stuff would end up under a motorhome parked on the kerb. And even when no disaster happened, it just felt completely different than it did in my imagination. It simply didn't feel like it had anything to do with me.

I experienced this during my Happiness Project, when I tried to 'enjoy the little things in life'. When I hear this phrase, I immediately think of that photo all women's magazines use whenever they talk about 'being good to yourself': a bath, with tea lights and rose petals on the side, with a woman with done-up hair who is blissfully stretching out in the bubbles. The caption tells you what to put into the water, and it is mostly some lavender-aloe-bio-herb-butter-oil. *Deeply nourishing for your skin and your soul.*

Now then, I am quite receptive to pictures like that, so as a result I end up in pretty little shops with shelves full of colourful liquids, salts and bath balls. I decide to buy a facial mask and a rose-scented bath oil, supposed to soften my cellulite skin to baby smoothness. I also buy, for good measure, a natural sponge. Once I sit in the tub, I can squeeze it over my shoulders in a very attractive way. I even buy rose petals, because this 'me time' is supposed to be exactly like the picture in the magazine, and my imagination.

Sunday night is the night. I have *a date with myself* –

that is what us spa specialists call this kind of time. I put a magazine on the little shelf where I also keep the shampoo bottles, place the tea lights and the rose petals along the sides of the tub, and run the bath with the rose oil. Unfortunately, it doesn't bubble, but it smells really good. It also looks very pretty. I put up my hair and step into the water, lie around a bit and move the natural sponge up and down my arms and legs a few times. It gets a bit boring after that. I manage to grab the magazine and start to turn the pages, squinting, because tea lights don't give off as much light as you might have thought. Then, accidentally, I push one of them off the tub with my elbow, and now the bath mat is covered in wax, but at least it hasn't caught fire. Relieved, I lean back.

While the hair clip is digging into my scalp, I notice that the body parts not covered by warm water get cold rather quickly. That is annoying, and I give in to the urge to sink one arm into the warmth. My hand gets wet, too, and immediately soaks the right-hand pages of the magazine, and now I can't turn the pages any more. The water itself gets cooler, too. So far, I am not finding this 'me time' particularly relaxing so I shove a few wilted rose petals into the water – but then it does get a bit more exciting.

Have you ever tried to get bath oil out of your hair? You can wash it three times, but it still looks like you want to take part in an oily hair competition – with a good chance you'll win it. Then you get out and, with a towel wrapped around your head, you are already feeling quite tense, but on it goes, because now you are trying to remove the oily film containing all the shaved-off leg stubble from the sides of the bath. Don't panic when you see the bloody spots on your body; that's only the squishy rose petals clinging to your skin. I have never had a bath as stressful as this.[3]

What to do? I am not the woman in the photo. I also am not the one whose Christmas presents are always lovingly decorated and creatively wrapped.

The same applies to more profound changes, when, for example, you don't only want a bath, but maybe wish for more success, to be more positive or more extroverted – something far-reaching and different. This urge supports a whole industry that offers a weekend course for each and every unloved characteristic. Do you want to have a fascinating personality? It will cost you 300 quid and can be achieved in only one single weekend. With the help of 'highly effective methods', just in case you were wondering how that might work.[4]

Have you ever attended a workshop? Or a seminar or a retreat? Or a weekend-intensive coaching course? Anything to somehow improve yourself on a personal level? I have attended quite a few, mostly for research, and I haven't always been successful. Given the number of courses I

---

3 A version of the previous two paragraphs first appeared in Das Glücksprojekt: Wie ich (fast) alles versucht habe, der glücklichste Mensch der Welt zu werden, mvg Verlag, ISBN-13:978-3868822052

4 http://www.personal-power-coaching.de/SeminarFaszinierendePersoenlichkeit.php

have attended, I should now be a very positive person and filthy rich; I should communicate without violence and I should have met my guardian angel.

Some of these courses have been recommended to me by others, for example, the one with the guardian angels (Anne) or the one about communication without violence (L.), but I like going, though rather out of interest than because of a personal need. If you toy with the idea of booking such a course because you have a sense that there is something not quite right with your soul, don't! You will only meet sad people, who will cry far too much and too often. Most participants attending such events regularly are true experts when it comes to their favourite topic. I may be wrong, but if those workshops for gaining inner peace and positivity worked, people would cry less and dance more ...

Introvert, shy Imogen will not turn into a dancing Denise, and the small one from the IT department will not turn into an enchanting Don Juan after a Chatting-up Course for Champions. A very lovely shaman woman who ran a course on the topic 'The Inner Power Animal' (parrot, just in case you were wondering) said that most participants were suffering from low self-esteem. But most people suffer from low self-esteem. In fact, pretty much everybody I know does – apart from, maybe, Donald Trump and my friend Ole.

Whatever weaknesses we might be harbouring, they will

probably remain with us. We will not turn into butterflies. Muddling through is real life. This completely imperfect life with all its insecurities and brimming bookshelves and the tired sex life ... that is our life, it has been for a while and it cannot be stopped. *Es lo que hay* – 'that's all there is', as they say in Spain, as if life were a bowl of soup someone has put in front of us. But we are forever fascinated by people who have not gone under, even after a terrible blow. It gives us some hope that *we can really achieve something if only we would make enough of an effort.*

When we hear such success stories, we are always told that they should give us hope. But research has shown that people often return to their 'normal' level of life satisfaction after a setback. It seems that we are born that way. It works in both directions, whether it is a car crash or a lottery win. You simply have to accept it. You will not achieve everything, even if you make a hell of an effort. But it is not just you; it's true for everyone.

'You can get it if you really want' versus 'You can't always get what you want'

There are a hell of a lot of things we cannot influence. There are losses that will always hurt. Depression is often chronic and untreatable. Some people have a tendency to choose unhealthy partners or drugs. In addition, we cannot change relatives, and sometimes not our boss or workmates. Life is not fair, and very often it is a bitch, and that won't change either. As much as you might wish your mother or your boss would be more or less ... *something*, and for yourself to be less or more ... *something*, it will not happen. Despite this, some of these impossible wishes top the list of the things we want to achieve. Maybe, if we made more of an effort, worked out our past, understood better the why ... But this is a fallacy.

Admit it. I had to, too. In order to change L. – and I don't mean his tendency to spread dirty socks on the floor around the bed, rather than putting them into the laundry basket, as if he wanted to create a magic sock circle – I would have to operate on his frontal cortex. And I am reluctant to do this.

Seriously, it doesn't work. We need to accept that we are as we are, and that our possibilities are limited. This doesn't only mean no decorated pinecones on my Christmas presents, but also – and this is a more painful insight – that I won't turn into the open, curious, positive and gregarious person I would like to be.

This is very difficult, but when someone asks me what I like doing in my spare time, I could answer:

I like playing tennis and sometimes I go sailing with my friends. I also volunteer in an animal shelter and do an advanced course in Italian, but I sometimes like being on my own in my chic penthouse, reading the latest books, and then I meet up with my numerous friends to have a vegan meal.

But that is a lie.

I would have to say:

In my free time I like wearing jogging bottoms and staying at home.

I am not particularly interested in meeting new people, because I find the ones I know demanding enough. I don't even like going on holiday: as I said, I like being at home in my jogging bottoms. I am as I am, and I won't change anything about it in a fundamental way – and not for other people, either.

But what I can stop doing is putting pressure on myself or feeling bad about the fact that I am this way or that way, and not how I would like to be. I can stop worrying about the things I cannot change, and instead concentrate on things I am actually very good at.

Instead of wishing that your difficult parents would change, you could maybe learn to establish a peaceful way of dealing with them. Instead of permanently feeling bad because your life is not filled with love and happiness, it would be a more realistic goal to simply be proud of how you are coping anyway.

And that is the reason why, after a fun-filled night with alcohol and cigarettes, I don't feel bad any more, and I don't think: '*God, I smoked again! I feel terrible that I can't give up properly!*' Instead I enjoy the evening and have an agreement with myself to look after myself and not overdo it. Instead of the ubiquitous '*I will love myself more*', I'd rather say, *'I find the efforts I am making to enhance my well-being quite impressive!'*

Once you understand that self-improvement has its limits, you can learn how to deal with these limitations better. This is much more efficient than permanently crying about the fact that this or that isn't working. Just don't give a toss about it!

Here's a list of things that we don't have much power over, but we still have a sense that we should modify or change them:

- Income
- The need to stay at home wearing jogging bottoms
- What other people think or feel about you
- The fact that you can't stop hating (or loving) X
- The state of the relationship
- Being an introvert
- Control over the problem of X
- The fact that your partner is a workaholic
- The fact that your brother has an addiction
- The fact that your children are ....
  ....
  ....

Tick the issues concerning you and add some to the list. Then, you and me, we will lean back and not give a crap about all this self-improvement any more.

Isn't that absolutely wonderful? The idea that there is nothing you should improve? No pushing yourself, no kicking yourself, no expectations, no 'I have to work on that' or 'I have to change this'!

Because we don't have to. Things will be all right. Caterpillars are lovely creatures.

Things to not give a damn about

It is a very satisfying feeling to say goodbye to certain ideas and notions, such as the concepts of ourselves and images that seem desirable, shaped by what society presents us as the ideal. Pursuing an ideal only creates negative feelings: guilt, bad conscience, complexes, low self-esteem. Don't give a shit about ideals; we want positive feelings instead.

However, abstract concepts like ideals can be difficult to pin down. If you are still a beginner when it comes to cutting out negative aspects of your life, maybe start by getting rid of some of your 'things'.

Things are wonderfully suited to be ruthless about, simply because you cannot hurt their feelings. In normal life, we have a lot of things. Has Auntie Meg, rest her soul, left you a fox fur stole? Did that dreadful Swarovski chandelier cost you a fortune? Do you have an array of hardly used fitness gadgets in the garage? Fantastic! Possessions are truly wonderful – but only the ones we really use, or which give us a good feeling. As much as you liked Auntie Meg, you probably don't like her fox stole at all – arghhh, those creepy fake glass eyes! What we are suggesting in this chapter about not giving a toss has nothing to do with Auntie Meg herself, bless her, or the dead fox, or the rowing machine. It has to do with the reasons why we own these things. It's quite possible that once you start thinking about this, the odd object, garment or gadget will get thrown out with force.

Here are some reasons why you should keep something:

- It makes you smile when you look at it
- You use it

That's all. With those two criteria at hand, have a look around your house. In case you are looking at your partner now, don't! Partners aren't things. They will be investigated under the heading 'Love' on page 160. Bring him/her back in now!

If you spot something you are not sure about, do the following test. If one of the following reasons for keeping it applies, throw it out:

Reasons to get rid of things:

- Because it is still just about OK and just about works
- Because it was a gift
- Because you have never thrown out heirlooms
- Because it might come in handy one day

- Because you might like it again one day
- Because it was expensive
- Because it might become fashionable again
- Because it is fashionable
- Because you would feel guilty if you threw it out
- Because you have always had it
- Because throwing it out will be followed by seven years of bad luck

This also applies to the contents of your wardrobe and the shoe cupboard. For most people, 40 per cent of this can be divided up into things that:

- Do not fit
- Will definitely fit one day when you have managed this issue with dieting and exercise

But we have done with that already.

If you stick to these rules, you may find that the expensive designer blazer will go, but the pretty leather corsage or Granny's impossible wedding dress will stay, because every time I look at those, I remember a very, very funny evening, and it might have to do with the fact that L. was wearing the wedding dress.

The category 'things' contains all sorts of objects but also abstract stuff, like, for example, the correct use of the split infinitive, something I really, really don't give a toss about, or sticking to rules such as 'no red wine with fish'. My main rule here is: 'As long as it tastes OK, you can drink it.' The fish, after all, doesn't notice what kind of coloured liquid now surrounds it. 'Things' also include politics, local, national and international – even though they involve real, living people. But politics is a 'thing' that I have decided not to get in touch with very often.

Here is now a selection of annoying things that I really don't give a damn about. Be inspired! You will have a whole page to write down all the things you can think of and that you, from now on, won't give a toss about any more either.

Media furore regarding American presidential elections

Isn't it a crazy spectacle? Some two years ahead of the actual event you are being bombarded with information about the most absurd candidates for the highest post in the USA. And I actually take notice of that!

I have no idea why my brain wastes space for me to know not only who is the president of the United States and not only who would like to *become* the president and is now a candidate. No, I even know which arseholes are vying to become a *candidate*! And why? Who knows how much brain space this Donald Trump occupies now, and how many important bits of information are excluded? If I didn't take all this in, maybe I would now know the difference between amphibians and reptiles. Or I could remember my first teacher.

Loving sport

Nobody can claim I didn't try. I have played volleyball, been jogging, gone to fitness classes, had a personal trainer and have allowed a very fit young policeman to hold me in a headlock during martial arts. (Actually, that wasn't that bad at all.) But sport in general, I must concede, is not for me. For a long time, I was embarrassed to make such a statement, as I firmly believed that EVERYBODY on this planet apart from me does some sort of exercise and loves it. Oh, to be able to run through the park like those lithe and fit girls – that was my ideal. But about this ideal, together with all the other sweating joggers, I now don't care – I smile and savour another piece of chocolate.

Beards

Seriously, what is the point?

If you meet a guy with a full beard, he might look quite passable – but who knows whether he would still be handsome without it? A man with full facial hair is a cat in the bag. A very hairy bag. And eventually you might discover this cat is as ugly as the night is black. You simply don't know.

Tapas

I have never grasped the concept of tapas. I understand that it is great to get a small snack with your beer – of course it is. What I don't understand is when friends say: 'Hey, let's go for some tapas!'

You sit in front of tiny plates with very little on them, and the whole group will want a taste. In the end you pay as much as for a big Argentinian steak but you are still hungry.

Alternative tourism

I have no idea why some people are dying to go to places where there are no tourists. In my experience, there are always quite good reasons why tourists are in popular places – on a clean beach, for example, or at an architectural landmark, or close to a beautiful landscape. Of course, one can always go and see places where nobody has ever set foot: the industrial area, for example, or a few really dark alleyways in dodgy neighbourhoods. Or on the part of the coast where they get rid of the sewage. It's more adventurous, sure, but it's not very nice. I have always felt a bit 'uncool' with this opinion, but I don't give two hoots any more. I am like a sheep. I want to go where everyone else is going.

EastEnders and Corrie

Can someone please explain to me the difference?

Friends, Acquaintances and Strangers

- Strangers
- Acquaintances
- Friends

As long as you are busy attempting not to care about the size of your own bum, your own savings account or your own meagre self-esteem, you are still at the beginner's level. This will prepare us for the real tests in the future. Because as soon as other people get involved, we move to Level 2. Ideally, you are quite sussed now and have been successful in not giving a toss about a few things. Maybe you have given up ironing (you don't give a crap about creases), maybe you have stopped wearing those terribly uncomfortable bras that create a lovely cleavage (you don't give a damn about your cleavage), and if I am unlucky, you have thrown out this book (you don't give a shit about self-help books). If I'm in luck, you are ready for Level 2: other people.

Strangers are the easiest group of other people to deal with.

Strangers

Generally, strangers are not a problem at all. Strangers only become a problem when they involve an alleged rich uncle in Nigeria, a salesman on your doorstep wanting to flog double-glazing or a guy on the phone trying to sell insurance. For many admirable people, those strangers are not an issue at all. They get rid of them in such a cool and confident way that I can't help being impressed. They shall be praised; they are our role models.

But if you even harbour a slight trace of a wish to please everyone, and you want to be liked by your boss, by your doctor and, please, also by the grumpy waiter in the pizzeria next door, then this chapter is for you. We are a lovable bunch, really, but unfortunately a little helpless when challenged to stand our ground. Against anybody, really. We are the weakest link in the chain of pedestrians and get immediately recognised by the charity fundraisers who urge us to sign up for regular contributions. And by Jehovah's Witnesses. A harmless shopping trip means running the gauntlet, and no matter if you just wanted to do some relaxed window-shopping, when you encounter all those people wielding a clipboard or a collection box, you put your head down and rush on as if hurrying to the nearest A&E unit. A leisurely walk turns into a marathon. I have managed to get through the pedestrian area in my hometown during the Christmas high season of charity fundraising in under four minutes.

But explain that when you come home:

'Have you checked out this or that?'

'Did you get this or that?'

'No ... er ... I had no time.'

'???'

But you are not even safe at home. My front door seems to have something written on it in invisible ink. For the charity fundraisers it seems to say, in bright neon letters: 'Ask here for donations for your organisation, project or whatever you might want. Don't be put off by an initial "no". The petite brunette will give you whatever you want.'

Some charities, it seems, send their new fundraisers to me first to give them a bit of confidence. It took years until the Jehovahs eventually stopped calling, because, in the end, I think they felt sorry for me.

On the phone it isn't much better. I have come up with the most elaborate excuses and justifications, so that someone trying to sell me a new phone contract once actually hung up on me. I nearly rang him back, because that was very rude!

But it *is* rude. And to hammer that into my brain – maybe yours as well – I have asked myself the following questions:

1. Am I generally happy to donate?
2. If yes, for what and in what way?
3. Do I really need some subscription or a new phone/internet provider/electricity contract?
4. Do I wish to help the marketing department of the company by answering some questions?
5. Do I like to negotiate a contract by telephone?
6. Do I personally harm someone when I reject the offer?

It is possible that by answering those questions you end up with a totally different result to me, and you'll find that you urgently need some new magazine subscriptions or that you like the way that the fundraisers talk you into donating. But if your answers are like mine, it will look like this:

1. Yes.
2. Don't know, and online.
3. No.
4. Under no circumstances.
5. No!
6. No, I don't think so.

From that point on, there is only a short path towards not giving a toss about strangers:

Step 1: Choose an organisation you wish to donate to

Get some information online or from the press about the aims and practices of some organisations. The issues are too numerous to list. You know what's important to you.

Step 2: Donate

It is easiest to donate a fixed sum annually at a certain date, maybe when your tax return is due, or monthly, going straight out of your bank by direct debit.

Step 3: To all the others who don't know how you have organised this, explain it when necessary ...

... but not to the old man with the dog who always sits at the supermarket entrance.

The only thing that still makes you vulnerable is pity. The poor student, who does it as a part-time job and must meet his quota, the nice guy selling double-glazing in his ill-fitting suit who has a blind ex-wife in a wheelchair and two sick mothers – what can you say to them without appearing hard-nosed and callous? How about: 'One question – if I have a little financial crisis in the future, maybe because I have not said *no* often enough to people like you, could I come to you for help? Could I just visit you and explain my personal situation, and would you be so kind as to help me out? What, you don't want me to come and see you at home? Oh, so you don't seem to like it when strangers ring your doorbell and want money from you? Well, well. You sound just like me, then.'

You don't even have to say it aloud; it is the thought that will change your attitude. Since it dawned on me that I am not allowed to ring the telephone guy or the electricity people at home and that the man with the double-glazing would be outraged if I turned up on his doorstep, I slam my front door with such force that its hinges quiver.

And without the slightest trace of a bad conscience. Don't give a damn about a bad conscience.

(A word of warning in case you are a bit short-sighted: if you notice, while slamming the door shut, that the person on the other side is extremely small and it is the end of October, it might be kids doing 'Trick or Treat'.)

Landlords are also part of the group of strangers – I might have met him or her, but never got to know them. If they visit unannounced, I slam the door, just as with the poor trick-or-treat kids. (I will end up in hell, I know.) Our landlords have inherited the house we currently live in and some other ones as well, which is why I find them annoying – just because they have inherited houses and I haven't. In addition, we pay them a monthly sum, and I don't like that either. I have no idea what the landlords do with the rent money, I suppose they have expensive hobbies like island collecting or something, because one thing is clear: they do not invest any money in the upkeep of their houses. At least not voluntarily. If you are persistent (and, God knows, I can be very persistent when the roof is leaking) they will consider some repairs. But not before they have stomped through our house on three consecutive Sundays with various tradespeople, and then given the contract to the cheapest with the uninsured cowboy builders. I don't like them, these landlords. L. remains completely at ease with them and doesn't understand my rage, which is why I feel even more like a madwoman who defends her front door against the baddies: 'It is my house. Go away!' But it is theirs, unfortunately.

But then something amazing happens: as soon as the landlord and the tradespeople have arranged with me to check the place, I turn into a high priestess of cleanliness. I move furniture, tidy up, dust and mop like it is a real pleasure. And why? So that it looks nice when the landlord comes visiting. *And why?* I haven't the faintest idea. Is it a kind of vassal identity complex?

The next time a landlord visit is due (because the heating is leaking) I will force myself not to check all the rooms beforehand, and instead I will sit on the sofa, totally relaxed, and read a good book (which doesn't work very well when you're trying hard to ignore all the dusty nooks and crannies for dust). 'I don't give a toss what the landlord thinks of us,' I will say to L. confidently, and then the doorbell will go, and they will have arrived, the arses.

The meaning of this behaviour is clear: it is not at all about the fear that the landlord might think badly of us or could even cancel the tenancy because the bedroom floor is littered with L.'s socks. The point is, landlords are not close friends, and I don't want them to see our socks or other dirty laundry. I don't even want them to see our bedroom. That is also the reason why my mother always thoroughly cleans the house before the cleaning lady arrives. She doesn't want to share her intimate spaces with strangers. My dirt is mine! I think the same. *My* socks (well, L.'s), *my* house – piss off!

If you come to visit, though, and the place looks like a pigsty, then you can be sure that you are very welcome. You are with friends!

Sometimes you need to clearly define what exactly you don't want to care about any more, so that you can live the life you want to. In this case, don't do that thing of pretending not to care – in other words, care!

Now, think about how much stress strangers in your life cause you. What kind of stress is it? Would you do those people any harm if you didn't give a damn about them or what they represent?

Strangers who cause you stress: ....
Kind of stress: ....

Should you give a toss about them? Yes / No

It's working! Keep at it: this will get better and better with practice!

Acquaintances

Not giving a damn about strangers is the easiest of the tasks in this chapter. It is more difficult with *acquaintances*. They are a blessing and a curse all in one. Acquaintances are people you regularly meet in the supermarket, in yoga classes, when travelling. Acquaintances are Ben's dad from the nursery, a neighbour, someone giving you a lift to work or someone you dance a night away with. The good thing about acquaintances is that they don't know you as well as friends do. That is quite a lovely advantage, because, for one thing, you can pretend to be much funnier, more charming, lovable or daring than you really are. You can play-act any role – as long as you are slightly pissed. You can practically try on a different outfit to see what it would feel like to be someone else or be at least somewhat different. You can do this with friends too, of course, and it can be quite funny, but the biggest advantage of acquaintances is something else: just because they don't know you well, they will look at you with a clear mind and without prejudice. If I tell my dear friend Jana, for example, how annoying my job in the advertising agency is, because client X doesn't like my concept for haemorrhoid cream, she can, because of our old friendship, dig up the whole history and tell me about all the positive aspects of my job. She will also remind me of how often my concepts are successful. That is truly wonderful. But from somebody without this background knowledge I get completely different comments, such as:

- So what would happen if you just ditched advertising completely?
- Can you really justify it to yourself, when you ...
- What can possibly be good about haemorrhoid cream?
- Is client X a complete idiot?

Sometimes, when you and your best friend become blind to the shortcomings of the job, acquaintances can give you new ideas and impulses you wouldn't come up with yourself. All you need to do is pluck up the courage to answer honestly when asked: 'How's things?' The conversation that comes afterwards can be really productive.

So far, though, we have only mentioned the 'good' acquaintances. The ones we really don't want to have to care about any more are the Category 2 ones, the bad acquaintances.

Sandra, for example, is a former colleague who always gets in touch when she needs something. Sandra doesn't understand Photoshop. Sandra needs a babysitter. Sandra has a few questions regarding her tax return. Sandra wants my advice for her website and, oh yes, she is moving house next week, could I come and help?

Or Stefan, who constantly moans and groans about how bad the world is. You go out for an ice cream, all relaxed and happy, and have to listen to his complaints about how expensive the ice cream is and how cheap it used to be, and how the owner probably has to pay protection money to the mafia, and Berlusconi and blah blah blah, and how bad sugar is for you, and the modern diet in general, and then there's the abattoirs! The cassata gets stuck in your throat.

I also need to mention Mireille, a Frenchwoman with a very cute accent, but a demanding personality, where every group she joins turns into a one-woman show. The name of this stage play is the same each and every time: *Mireille*.

Also in this group is Hannah's new friend, and Hannah is so much in love with him that you only ever see her profile, because she looks at him constantly. He is very good-looking and very charming ... but the way he puts Hannah down is unbearable.

I could go on and on, and it seems there is a huge pool of real dicks in the world, and it also seems as if they all turn up in *my* life at some point. In yours, too? What a coincidence!

I don't know how you handle this, but my strategy for dealing with acquaintances of this category only consists of such techniques as those on the next page!

Have you ticked at least two boxes on there?

	I do too:
Not answer the phone	
If I answer the phone, I wave my hand in front of my face so technically, it makes a draft	
Invent an excuse	
Try to remember my excuse from last time	
When outside, pretend blind or deaf when the doorbell rings, be very quiet and wait – unless it is the pizza delivery	

Congratulations, you are just as stupid as I am. Why are you doing all this when you can simply say 'No' to Sandra's cries for help or not allow Stefan to spoil your ice cream? Experts say it is because of low self-esteem. I say because it is *awkward*. The experts are presumably right.

What Sandra, Stefan, Mireille and Hannah's friend have in common is their negative effect on you. You feel annoyed or downright unwell in their presence, and that saps a lot of energy. If all these people suddenly disappeared from my life in a big bang, I wouldn't be sad – maybe I would even go for an ice cream to celebrate. But it is very strange indeed that we don't do anything ourselves to eliminate them from our lives with a big bang! Quite the opposite. While Stefan rants about the spiritual abyss of Italian politics and politicians in general, I meekly nod like a sheep and listen to all this nonsense. Afterwards I have a quick look at Sandra's website for her, and who will come and meet us tonight in Café Pimpernel? Exactly: Mireille, the stupid cow.

'Why am I doing this?' I ask L. that night while sitting at my desk and staring at Sandra's website.

'Because you are a coward, darling!' I hear from the kitchen, where L. is busy cooking with our boy, where a glass of red wine is waiting and where I'd rather be.

'Mummy coward!' my son repeats, and then they giggle a bit.

Something is not right here.

Apparently, the urge of wanting to please other people is quite normal. It has to do with the fact that we are herd animals. Even very young children understand this basic impulse: 'I need other people. Better not mess it up with them.' Ten thousand years ago, you needed to be part of a tribe in order to survive. You had to deal with sabre-tooth tigers and kill mammoths and you needed a group to do that. You can't achieve things like that on your own. It made perfect sense not to mess it up with all the others, because expulsion from the tribe meant certain death. This mechanism is still working in us, despite pizza deliveries, and we have long since dealt with sabre-tooth tigers quite successfully. Wanting to be part of a community is in our genes, and it is a good thing, because it diminishes the risk of turning into a psychopath.

But honestly, has Sandra ever helped me to kill a mammoth? And I have no idea what Stefan would do should he ever come across a sabre-tooth tiger. Would he talk him into a deep depression? No, the reality and my behaviour are just like my ex and me: we simply don't fit.

This is completely absurd. The aim of my behaviour, say the experts, is wanting to please and to inspire love and respect – things like that. But when I look around I prefer people who say honestly what they think, who do what they deem right, even at the risk that someone might find them stupid. The experts have a prompt explanation for this too, one that is supposed to encourage me in future situations: 'A lion does not care what the sheep are thinking of him!'

This lioness, however, still stares at Sandra's website and gets increasingly grumpy. I tiptoe to the kitchen, and there is my son with a big smile. He is holding a large wooden spoon, and there are splashes of tomato sauce all over him. 'Well?' says L., also with a smile. He reaches out for me. 'Have you finished?'

I haven't. Sandra's thing is a botched-up free website template that has been carelessly adapted. It is fussy, ugly and littered with typos. I have no idea where to start.

'I don't even know where to begin,' I complain and put my head on L.'s shoulder.

'Mummy sad?' asks my son, slightly worried, and puts his little hand on my arm as comfort. That is the final straw. My child wants to comfort me because I can't get it together to say no to some stupid woman who is not even my friend? Am I mad? I kiss my man and my child and grab my glass of wine.

'I am a lion!' I announce and go to the phone. 'Roaarrrr!' the two of them growl, and I am smiling again.

While dialling, I shout a loud *roaarrrr* and take a deep breath.

'Yes?'

'Hello, Sandra! Hey, I just want to tell you, well, the thing with your website. I had a look at it and ... quite honestly ... it's too much for me.'

'How do you mean?'

'Well, it's too much work.'

'Well, so what am I supposed to do now?'

'I have no idea. What are you doing at the moment?'

When people come up with such an abominable response it is much easier to send them packing. Our call is over rather quickly, and suddenly I am not sitting at my desk any more, sulking, but am in the kitchen with my man and my child. I lay the table while we make lion sounds. Do I feel bad about it? A little bit, yes. But when rationally analysing the facts and the result, I find that it was absolutely the right thing to do, and now I take a few dancing steps and I don't – *olé* – give a damn about my guilty conscience. Hours of work versus playing lions with my son. I should have started this project ages ago.

'I couldn't come to terms any more with the fact that somebody would take away time and energy from the little one, from you and from us,' I say to L. when we are in bed later.

But I am not quite happy. 'It took you two to make me do it. I should be able to make such decisions by myself,' I go on, but L. is yawning already and touches my face.

'It doesn't matter how and when it happens, the main thing is that you are on fire – isn't it?'

He is right. I'm on fire.

I am not sure the experts would be entirely happy with this statement though. It is not the 'correct' solution; I have cheated. It is, after all, about bolstering my self-esteem. And – hello? – where is my team of experts all of a sudden? I think maybe I just haven't given the slightest toss about them. Then I drop off and sleep like a baby.

The next evening in Café Pimpernel it gets really tough. My dear friend Anne can't come, and Jana is on time at eight, but has to leave for home half an hour later because she has a bad cold. The one who doesn't go home early is Mireille. She is on top form, positioning herself right next to me, sipping her drink, and while talking to me she is permanently looking over my shoulder. When I turn around, there is only the door behind me – she is simply keen to see who else is coming in. Every now and then she looks into the big mirror behind the bar and pulls some strands of hair either about her face or behind her ear. When people behave like that, you feel like a human prop.

'Hey!' we suddenly hear from a table in the corner, and there is Hannah with her Clooney Clone in tow. The evening can hardly get better. Only Sandra is missing, the old wingnut. But instead of leaving in a friendly but firm way, I docilely trot over to Hannah's table and introduce Mireille to the couple. 'Sit down!' Hannah beams.

'Oh, I meant to go ...' I really want to avoid all this, but Mireille puts a hand on my arm.

Hannah says: 'No way!' and points out my glass is still half full, so the next moment I find myself sitting down, inwardly shaking my head. But what happens then is very interesting.

Mireille is on top form. She looks as if someone has injected a mixture of Red Bull and cocaine directly into her veins. She frequently throws her head back, shakes her hair to one side or the other, laughs extra loud when Hannah's friend says something, and after every sip from her glass she licks her lips. It is very obvious: Mireille is on the pull. For outsiders, this is not a nice picture, but the effect is clear. Suddenly Clooney Clone is straightening up, he is talking in a louder voice and, I may be wrong, he has moved a little bit away from Hannah. Hannah's sensors are on high alert; she tries to compete with Mireille with similar hair gestures, talking too loudly and too much, and waving her hands and arms – but in vain. The catastrophe is unavoidable, at least for Hannah.

The next time Mireille's hair is flung into my eyes, I also notice that I am getting quite nervous myself, but not because of Clooney Clone. It is an automatic reaction that sets in every time some discord is developing somewhere. I find it so *awkward* that I immediately try everything I can to re-establish peace and harmony. In this case, the best strategy would be to knock Mireille out.

But as this is not an option because I want to stay out of jail, I am forced to just look on. The big surprise about this situation is that I suddenly realise it doesn't matter one single bit whether I am nervously rocking my foot, squirming inside or getting a stomach ulcer out of shame for the others – or whether I lean back and wait patiently until this circus is over. My suffering is not helping Hannah in the slightest, and nobody else either. I am not responsible for this disaster, not for Hannah and not at all for Mireille, and that is why I don't have to apologise for having introduced her in the first place. They are all grown-ups and can play on their own. It is another really lovely and liberating feeling, and it comes as a big surprise.

I am not responsible.

That feeling is so great that I keep pondering it a few more times.

That said, I do feel sorry for Hannah; it is a massacre. Mireille doesn't take prisoners. After twenty minutes the new dream couple has arranged a date, to which Hannah is also invited – 'of course'. Yes, of COURSE!

When Mireille gets ready to go and Clooney Clone is so kind to offer her a lift home, I do the only thing I can do for Hannah: I put my arm around her and order two shots.

To feel responsible for others reaches a different level when it is about our friends. Oh, friends ...

Friends

Friendship is a very special phenomenon. It's like love, only different. There is an old proverb:

> Love asked friendship
> 'Why do you exist when there is me already?'
> And friendship answered:
> 'To bring a smile
> Where you leave tears.'

This is true. There is a significant difference between love and friendship.

A wise man once said that you can fall head over heels in love at ninety. But friendship is a kind of positive human state that takes time. You need to have had many a drink together, experienced things together and also have had the odd conflict. One needs to have suffered together and learned from each other.

Friends are more important for our happiness than love, more important for your health than exercise. Those one, two, three people you can tell everything to, and who you can rely on regardless, those who don't want anything else from you other than to make you happy – no, there aren't many of them. Quite a few people can cluster together, like teenagers around the village bus stop, but real friends, no, you won't have many. Not those kind of friends. The ones you can ring at four in the morning from your ex-boyfriend's place and say: 'Can you pick me up?' even when his place is in a different country. And they won't ask: 'Erm ... Costa Rica? Are you mad?' but: 'Where exactly is Costa Rica?'

Counting my friends is very easy, because I don't have that many. Maybe this sounds a bit arsey, but that's the truth. (I could count L. because, by God, we have had conflicts.)

One of my two best friends you have already met a few pages ago. I have known her since I was five. Anne, the friend with the eso-mania. If I met Anne today, I would not give her a second glance. This esoteric stuff really gets on my nerves with other people. But not with Anne. Why? Maybe because I feel that I know her inside out. The person she is, her nature. And this nature is wonderful – no matter how many energy-loading crystals she is wearing around her neck, I will always see Anne and not this eso-woman. Is that what is so special in old friendships? That you get to know the person before they take on a different attitude, a different costume, and then they don't even recognise themselves any more? Before they start to pretend to others and, with time, believe their new identity and lose themselves?

My other friend is Jana. I met Jana at university. I noticed her on the very first day, because she was wearing a T-shirt with the logo: 'No tits but wits'. We got on like a house on fire.

Over the years there were others, but they came and went, as through a revolving door. Jana stayed. I am sure that there are more people out there who I could be friends with. Maybe it is inertia that prevents us from discovering new people. Friends mean spending energy, after all. Sometimes I have the feeling that Anne and Jana are enough for me and I have no further capacity for more friends. I feel responsible for those two, and also for L., and, of course, my son. If they are not well, I'm not well. I would shoot off any time to pick them up wherever they are, even from the other end of the world. I guess that is the very opposite of not giving a toss.

It is through the friendship of my loved ones that I have learnt something valuable about helping. Helping itself is a wonderful thing, particularly when it is selfless and done with honourable aims. But whatever is well meant is not necessarily well done, and the best intention often turns into exactly the opposite. In the course of history, clear evidence for this is all the missionaries, armies and opiates that brought death to the people – but supposedly came to help.

Probably everybody knows the urge to help those who are suffering. If the person who is suffering is close to you, even more so. But help is not always helpful, and you only learn this when your attempts to be useful don't lead anywhere. That was the case with me and Anne. She suffers from depression.

How to avoid helper syndrome

When Anne told me that it wasn't simply days of bad mood but a real, full-on depression, I was the first to roll up my sleeves. I rubbed my hands and said: 'Well, what are we waiting for? Let's tackle this shit together!'

But that, it turned out, wasn't the kind of help Anne needed from me. Generally, in the initial stages of helping, one doesn't think much about the '*how*', one just starts acting. That isn't always a good idea. The more I tried to lift Anne's mood, the guiltier Anne felt because it didn't work, and the guiltier I felt that I hadn't succeeded. It made Anne worse, and we soon were in a vicious circle of guilt and pain, and that didn't help anybody. Up to this point, I had invested a lot of energy, time (and a lot of L.'s time) and tons of alcohol, but Anne wasn't getting any better. We all felt worse. That is a bad result for a helper.

It got even worse when Jana got involved. She was getting worried because she observed how I was failing and then felt compelled to help *me*. It was chaotic – until finally a very clever person from a professional advice service asked me the wise question: 'Do you think you can manage your friend's feelings better than anyone else, including your friend?' Good point.

When I relinquished the responsibility for Anne and her depression, the situation changed immediately. From this moment on I was able to notice how Anne herself dealt with this awful illness, to admire her and to tell her that, and that actually helped Anne, because she could be proud of herself. Instead of feeling a failure because I couldn't make her happier, or incompetent because I didn't find the right method, we celebrated little positive steps and the good moments we could salvage from that difficult time. It also has shown me a different side of Anne, one that I respect enormously.

If you have a friend with depression or an addiction problem, a mother with dementia or other personal issues on that level, there is a letter template by the psychiatrist Michael Bennett and his daughter Sarah Bennett in their book *F*ck Feelings*:

> *Dear Self/Spouse/Desperate Beggar/Huddled*
> *Masses yearning to breathe freely,*

I feel unable to watch someone I like suffer/ cry/get down/drown in sorrow without thinking that there is always a way and that it's me who has to find it by making more of an effort/going on a pilgrimage to Lourdes/lending money for psychotherapy, but I know that this is not true. I will try to make you better, if possible, by being there for you or making you laugh but if that doesn't work, it doesn't mean that you or I have failed. I will admire you for continuing to shower/ take the rubbish out/face a new day.[5]

Annoying habits of friends

In most cases (thank God), the problem with friends is not rooted in a serious mental illness; it is simply that they can be seriously annoying. Not the people, mind, but some of the things that they do. That's a fact. Nobody is utterly and thoroughly adorable and enchanting, and, surprise, surprise, I am not an exception. I badly get on the nerves of my loved ones when I try to communicate in quotes from films. The problem is, only I know the films I am quoting from, and only I find them irresistibly funny. But they have to stomach it, my loved ones, and I am only half as bad as L. who for some unknown reason

---

5 Based on Michael Bennett, Sarah Bennett, *F*ck Feelings: One Shrink's Practical Advice for Managing all Life's Impossible Problems*, Simon & Schuster, ISBN-13:978-1476789996

very often talks with a Welsh lilt – or what he thinks is a Welsh lilt. He hasn't really got a clue. When I meet him in the pub he might greet me with a loud '*Croeso*'.[6] Eventually I got used to it ...

Habits like that don't hurt anybody and can be labelled 'lovable quirks'. Friends are not perfect, and where would we be if we couldn't be a bit generous with ourselves and other people? Is it OK to be annoyed by friends from time to time? Of course, it is! You annoy them too (see my example with the film quotes).

Anne, for example, has this eso-mania we have mentioned. But she also wants to be nice to us, with the consequence that now and then *things* turn up in our house. Coasters, for example, with a pretty geometric pattern called 'Flower of Life', which apparently has a harmonising effect. Or a glass cylinder with little stones in that are supposed to vitalise our drinking water (brilliant toy for my son), as well as a glass pyramid and various horrible figurines of guardian angels. That is annoying, and if you think it is sweet of Anne, it's because you haven't seen the angel figurines.

Jana, on the other hand, has a super power I call tunnel vision. Once she has formed an opinion about something or someone, she is capable of blocking out everything that might contradict it. It can be quite demanding.

---

6 Welsh for 'Welcome'.

The reasons friends are annoying are as different as people in general. How do you annoy your friends? Do you like to sing when you are pissed? Do you tend to make lots of puns while having a conversation? Do you embellish your stories a bit too much? Be brave, write down all your 'lovable quirks':

- ....
- ....
- ....
- ....
- ....

Very good. But never mind, none of us is perfect. And where is the line between a lovable quirk and an unbearable peculiarity?

One benchmark might be how other people are impacted by it. Does something annoying about a person make me roll my eyes or does it drive me so crazy that I waste a lot of energy and time on it? Eye-rolling is a part of friendship, one has to tolerate it. And in a good relationship the other person is also able to share it. You need to live with it. Guardian angels/coasters/water vitalisation versus eye- rolling is a fair deal. But it gets difficult when sitting at a poetry slam in Overton-under-Stickleback, an evening on which you are sacrificing time and energy but you really don't care about. Especially when you have lots of other things to do, even if one of those things is merely a little nap on the sofa. Your time, your desires, are important.

At this point, and before I tell you about a few quite wonderful activities that my friends have attempted to make me swap with a sofa nap, I have to make this statement:

I help my friends immediately when they are in a tight spot (see Costa Rica). No matter what they need in any emergency, they can get it from me. My time, my ear, my kidney, my money or a watertight alibi. No problem. What I am ruling out now are things I personally don't care about and when my personal absence is not a disaster for others. Those are the things I won't give a damn about. Like Tom's poetry slam.

Or:

Gigs

After A-levels, one really should say goodbye to all this. In sixth form, it was of course perfectly OK for Josh, Ole and Jack to play in a band and regularly ask us to distribute flyers and to come to their gigs somewhere in a sports hall. It was of course just as acceptable to go and clap and shriek very loudly, even though we were sometimes not quite sure whether one song had ended and the next one had started. But it was OK, because we didn't have anything else to do. No Facebook, no Twitter, no *Candy Crush*. And also, no work, no child, no household and no urge to just have a little nap. That has all changed, God knows (particularly the napping).

For those reasons, and because Josh, Ole and Jack by now are a dentist, a landscape architect and a couples' therapist respectively (and not international rock stars), and the thing with telling the songs apart hasn't changed fundamentally, well, for those reasons I don't want to stand in sports halls any more. Mainly because they always smell a bit musty. Don't get me wrong, I don't want to see Josh, Ole and Jack in an opera house or a private salon either. The location is not the problem; the problem is the music. One way of avoiding the dilemma is to pretend to have a full-time job. You can rely on that until you have a child, and then you don't have to pretend any more. That is one of the advantages of having children. But if you are determined not to give a toss any more about the unimportant things in life, then it is unavoidable to say:

'I would rather (*iron/sleep/flagellate myself*) than come to one of your gigs. You are lovely people, and I love you, but your music is (*mediocre/not my taste/ridiculous*).'

Moving house

This is another relic from the past. During my twenties it seemed as if somebody was moving house every weekend. During that phase, all the flat-sharers I knew swapped with each other endlessly to try out all the possible combinations, mostly because of internal conflicts about fridge shelves, sexual partners or washing-up and cleaning rotas. In those days, you could manage the house moves with a VW van, and everybody took one box, a plant pot and a bamboo table from upstairs down to the van and up again to the new flat. Then we all had a crate of beer in the new environment.

Friends and acquaintances, however, who by now have all well crossed over the threshold of their thirties and still ask whether you can help at the weekend to move house, have either changed their flat-sharing style (never the case) or haven't noticed that life has changed (always the case). Instead of one removal box and one Yucca plant and a bamboo table, the helpers are confronted with a fully furnished three-bedroom flat on the third floor. No lift. And the washing machine is coming too, clearly. If you want to avoid conflict, you can claim some sort of back problem, and everyone over the age of thirty will believe you, but openly not giving a toss is a better way.

'I would rather (*nap/work/shave my legs*) than help with your house move. You are lovely people, and I love you, but it is too much hard work for me. I need my weekend to recover, but you can come over for a beer and a lasagne afterwards.'

Projects

The word *projects* maybe doesn't quite describe it. Better: *projects where your help is required.* Everyone has something dear to their heart, and of course one asks around in one's circle of friends and acquaintances for support and help. Some fantastic achievements have been initiated like that. If someone asks you to come and help with collecting toads and you like the idea (and toads too) – go and get your bucket! If you always wanted to create websites for your friends because they have such wonderful ideas like a *Mother's Clothes Swap Café* or *Open Mic in the Bakery* or an *Animal Shelter for Poor Poets* (not pets, it's not a typo) – this is your time. Take lonely dogs for a walk, do some pottery ... the main thing is that your heart must be in it. If it isn't, though, and you don't want to hurt your animal-loving and pottering and poem-writing friends, then say:

'I really love you, but I'd rather (*iron/sleep/flagellate myself*) than (*collect toads/make pottery/walk dogs*). I feel bad about it, but I can't stand (*toads/pots/dogs*).'

Leisure activities

There is a wealth of leisure activities available these days. Most of them I don't like (see 'jogging bottoms and staying at home').

When friends want to convince you of a certain activity ('We are going ice-climbing, that'll be great!') they often wrongly assume that one doesn't know how much fun such an activity is, and they feel obliged to describe it in great detail. However, because I find it difficult to communicate how much fun my 'jogging bottoms on the sofa' activity is, I make a principle of my rejections.

'I don't do climbing. Not ice-climbing either. On principle.'

Just go through your own list of activities that you feel pressured to participate in and ask yourself how you truly feel about them. It has a great effect. If you refuse to automatically go along with everything you get all the time for the things that are really important to you. To support this, and when in doubt, ask yourself the following questions:

- Is my decision based on a vague feeling my friend won't like me any more if I am not keen on (*toads/ pottery/poetry slams*)?
  Yes / No

- Is my decision based on a vague feeling my friend might think that I don't like him/her any more if I am not keen on (*toads/pottery/poetry slams*)?
  Yes / No

- Am I assuming we're making a deal? If I go to the (*toads/pottery/poetry slam*) then he/she has to come to Zumba with me, even though he/she hates it?

Yes / No

- Do I have the feeling these things are simply a part of friendship, as it is often described and praised in poetry?

Yes / No

If your answer is *yes* in at least one case, then next time just say no!

3

Family

- The interviews with Auntie Mabel
- The mother-in-law
- Presents and heirlooms
- *That* uncle is not allowed to come
- Religion and politics
- Food
- Family traditions
- Disappointing the parents

The family offers many creative opportunities to be a bit of a dick. It's the Advanced Level for Pros. This is not surprising because, from day one, we get it hammered into our heads that blood is thicker than water and that we must invite our uncle, who is a member of the Britain First party and whom nobody can stand, to all family gatherings. But when we grow older we realise: no, we don't have to invite our fascist uncle. Nothing will happen, apart from him maybe shedding a few tears. We don't know. Thank God, but we will not be confronted by him.

But most of the time, things are more complicated and subtle. Only very few family members are politically objectionable. Rather, they tend to be sweet old dears with a few idiosyncrasies, quirks and habits that can drive you mad in no time at all. The rule of thumb is that the closer the family, the quicker one gets mad. For outsiders, the trigger is often not at all noticeable. While you yourself are already beyond redemption with rage, everybody else sounds in unison: 'Why? Your *mother/aunt/sister* is such a lovely person!' And while you are foaming at the mouth and barely managing to croak: 'No, not nice!' you need to be careful that they don't think you odd. Family members drag a long tail behind. It's the whole history of all the things they have ever done, said, or caused – and that is a powerful emotional charge.

Because feelings towards family members are so complicated, we need to clarify whether we are only objecting to a particular idiosyncrasy, or whether we are justified in applying a fully fledged boycott?

Here is an example of a quirk of a family member (my mother) that drives somebody (me) to despair.[7]

There is something about my mother that drives me to the edge and frazzles my nerves. It is so bad that I get goose bumps if I even talk about it. It is hell: she hums.

Pah! you will say, that is nothing, but remember what drives *you* crazy. I am sure there is something trivial to which everybody else would say: *Pah!* Mine is humming. Hm-hm-hm-hmmmm.

Hm. It is not very melodious, even if she is humming tunes. And that is the next problem. The choice of songs is beyond description. In the middle of summer, it will be 'Silent Night', directly followed by a medley from *The Magic Flute* or Johnny Cash's greatest hits. We also get supermarket jingles. It can be quite funny, I agree, but what drives me nuts about this humming is something completely different. It is WHEN she hums. Mum always hums when she doesn't want to say what she wants to say. It goes like this:

Mum: 'You should rinse the plates, they clean up better.'

Me: 'Not necessary with our dishwasher.'

Mum: 'Hm-hm-hm-hmmmmm.'

Me: 'Arghhh!'

Or:

Mum: 'This Rees-Mogg looks like a tax dodger.'

Me: 'But you can't tell by looks if someone dodges tax.'

---

7 From: A. Reinwarth, *Das Sinn-Des-Lebens-Projekt*. Mvg ISBN-13-978-3868822915

Mum: 'Hm-hm-hm-hm-hmmmm.'

Me: 'Arghhh!'

This is how discussions go with my mother, when we are of a different opinion. It doesn't matter at all what it is about. My mother hums about personal fashion preferences as well as political statements.

Mum: 'Is that what you will be wearing at the wedding?'

Me: 'Why? Don't you like it?'

Mum: 'Hm-hm-hm-hmmmm.'

Humming is also her strategy when there is an awkward social situation, for example when people argue in her presence. Or during an embarrassed silence. Go shopping with my mum and somehow embarrass the salesperson. In less than three seconds you will hear 'Bridge over Troubled Water' right next to you. Hummed.

What really drives me mad about this humming is not the choice of songs but what it is replacing. She dodges every kind of conflict, doesn't ever express her own opinion, but makes it perfectly clear with her humming that she doesn't agree.

It is an extension of a fundamental issue that I do not get at all. My mother avoids making decisions like the plague. No matter what they are about. This has the effect that she is never ever responsible for anything that doesn't work, doesn't taste good or is impossible. And then she has an opportunity to say that she always knew what would happen in the first place. A typical sentence of hers is: 'You should have made it/done it that way.' Oh, I could tear my hair out!

I have been trying to boycott Mum's avoidance strategy for years now, by being persistent:

Me: 'Shall I cook for us or would you rather go to the pizzeria?'

Mum: 'What would you rather do?'

Me: 'Well, I wanted to know what you would like.'

Mum: 'But do you want to cook? I don't mind.'

Me: 'Just say what you want.'

Mum: 'The pizzeria would be lovely ... but we can also cook here.'

These conversations can take quite a long time.

This example is about a quirk of my mother. But should I stop caring about her any more? Heavens, no! Can I do something, anything, so that I am no longer enraged by her humming? Definitely not. But I can talk to her and ask her and try to understand why she finds it so difficult to make decisions. Does the humming stop? No. But it becomes a little bit less annoying.

We cannot change most of our loved ones' quirks, and you can't change yourself so that they don't drive you up the wall any more. Relatives are a challenge, and once you accept it, you might stay more relaxed.

What you can change, though, is your own behaviour. In my case, for example, during my conversations with Auntie Mabel ...

The interviews with Auntie Mabel

As long as I can remember – and even before I got together with L. – my Auntie Mabel has annoyed me at every family gathering. When she switches her drink from coffee to liqueur, she also very abruptly changes her line of questioning:

'Such terrible pictures from the civil war ... oh yes,' she says, and then turns to me with her little glass in hand, as if the words 'civil war' had reminded her something to do with me. 'Have you got another boyfriend?' Right on cue, the whole crew turns around and looks in my direction in a pitying and interested manner.

Never mind what I answer, the situation never improves. If I say 'Yes' it is immediately followed by an inquisition:

- What's his name? (Asked by *that* uncle, to exclude a possible immigrant background)
- What does he do? (Does he earn his own money, or do you have to support him like the last loser?)
- How old is he? (To evaluate the marriage potential)
- And the worst: when are you bringing him home? (So that we can check all your statements out)

But if, at that time, my answer was 'No', it wouldn't make much difference, because what would follow would be a detailed analysis of the reasons why I was single and how I could change the no-boyfriend situation, followed by general suggestions about my outfits, my hairdo, my self-esteem, my age, my culinary skills and my fertility.

What I am describing here is a strategy by my Aunt Mabel to gain information. Is it annoying? Yes, but – hello? – is the main reason it's annoying maybe because it is about you? It couldn't be more personal, after all. But there is no need to completely freak out, denounce Auntie Mabel and leave the house. Auntie Mabel has her good sides, like the rest of the family (apart from *that* uncle).

How to stop her, though, without offending Auntie Mabel and then for ever being labelled 'hypersensitive' by the rest of the family? With friendliness. With friendliness you don't have to give a toss about a whole range of issues that cause an inner eye-rolling. Nobody will be cross with you (in case that still matters), as long as you are friendly:

Auntie Mabel: 'Have you got a new boyfriend?'

Answer: 'Ah, Auntie Mabel, let's not talk about my love life – how was your holiday, that is much more interesting.'

If somebody still carries on prodding, you can always go to the loo. When you return, the clan will have turned to their next favourite topic: how Granny thought she had a tumour when she was pregnant – or whatever old stories are forever chewed over in your family.

You don't need to be blunt – like in the legendary story about the woman whose relatives whispered to her at every family wedding: 'You'll be next!' which only ended when she started to say it back to them at funerals.

The mother-in-law

In most cases you don't only have your own wonderful family. No, together with your life partner you get his or her family as well – for free! While, of course, you can choose your life partner – thank God – this doesn't apply to his or her family. Sometimes you are lucky, and you get on like a house on fire. Sometimes you get on so well that after a separation you miss them more than your ex. But it is also very possible that you only get on so-so or not at all. It's often the case that this so-so disastrous relationship develops between a girlfriend and her partner's mother. For example, between me and L.'s mother. She is the only one who thoroughly deserves the Facebook status 'It's complicated'. As much as I would like her to like me, and as much as she would like to like me, we cannot ignore one thing: I have stolen her son. And she will never forgive me for that.

Even when we first met she ever so subtly indicated that

I was not her dream of an ideal daughter-in-law. We met in a restaurant, and after the first tentative introductions and some polite conversation between starter and main course, my future mother-in-law disappeared into the toilet and threw up like never before.

A lot has changed since then. We have got to know each other better, L. and I had a baby, and my mother-in-law doesn't vomit any more when we meet. But there isn't much love between us, my mother-in-law and me; we are too different. Despite this, every time she comes to visit I make a huge effort – presumably with the hope that she will eventually like me a bit better:

- I get rid of all the dried-up pot plants, so she won't think that I let her son and her grandson die of dehydration.
- I tidy up and clean the bathroom.
- I put the sheets on that she gave us for Christmas last year.
- I feign culinary competence by putting little pots of fresh herbs all over the kitchen.
- I get a lovely cake from the best shop.
- I take the photos down from the fridge of the last fancy dress party we attended, during which I, dressed up as a bee, fell asleep, completely sozzled, on the table. I replace them with some family shots.

- I get that macramé hanging thing from the attic she once gave us as a present.
- I see to it that L. doesn't spoil all these efforts by saying things like, 'Why is it so clean here?', 'What is all the green stuff doing in the kitchen?' or 'Where did you get this horrific crochet thing?'
- I put a bottle of prosecco in the fridge, which I can secretly swig when things are going badly. If they are going well, I can still offer her a glass.

Once she has arrived, I try to contribute to the conversation, even when it is about things I don't have a clue about, such as women's magazines, shopping or her acquaintances and their respective health problems.

But do you know what? If there is one thing in my life I really shouldn't care as much about, then it is this attempt to please my mother-in-law.

'What do you think?' I ask L., who to this day loves telling the story about when his mum and I first met. He shrugs. 'What exactly do you want to do?' But the question is a completely different one: what *not* to do any more is the difficulty.

When my mother-in-law announces her next visit, I don't do any of the things I have listed above. Apart from the bottle of prosecco – one never knows. But by now I also don't give a damn about this fake 'not tidying up' so I tidy a few things (those socks in the bedroom) away.

I don't do any cleaning, the macramé thing remains in

the attic, the pissed photo stays on the fridge, and I don't buy a cake either. Instead, I have a great plan. I won't pretend to her any more.

As soon as she arrives my little boy hijacks her. I do *not* try to distract him after a while, so Granny gets a break. Instead, I clear out the dishwasher (and fill it again), check my emails and make coffee. Those two will be busy until all the new children's books have been introduced. In my mind I give *The Gruffalo* (very popular with two-year-olds) a high-five. Granny holds out much longer than I thought. And when, on her knees, Granny's top half disappears into the play tent and only her bottom is sticking out, I involuntarily grin. It looks really sweet.

When she is finally ready for a break she looks a bit dishevelled, but very happy. She sits down with me at the kitchen table, and I pour her a cup of coffee. She doesn't seem to notice that the kitchen isn't super clean, and the macramé thing is missing. However, what she immediately spots, to my embarrassment, is the pissed bee photo on the fridge door. She points to it and looks at me questioningly: 'What is that?'

Have you ever experienced one of those moments when you'd rather say: 'Oh, somebody we kind of know', instead of: 'Me as a completely pissed bee'? It was such a moment. The headgear with the antennae that had slipped over my face would have made it credible – I would have got away with it.

'Don't give a toss about pleasing the mother-in-law,' I heard my inner voice say, so I told her the truth. At first, she didn't say anything, and then she leaned over and took a closer look at the photo. 'What is that on your face? Are those tights?'

Now I needed to take a closer look too. 'That's the antennae. I made them from stockings and put those long balloons inside, but they deflated very quickly.'

'Ah,' she says and takes another sip of coffee. That is all – she doesn't even raise her eyebrows. But then she notices something in the kitchen. 'Weren't there some plants here last time?' she asks, looking around.

'Yes,' I nod, 'but I've thrown them out.' Now she *does* raise her eyebrows. 'They never live long with me,' I explain, 'and in any case, they're never the herbs that L. needs for cooking. He always buys them fresh in the market.'

'You don't seem to do much cooking?' she asks, and again I feel a near irresistible urge to lie.

'No,' I manage to say and prepare myself for one of those silences, as if nothing had happened.

Instead, Granny laughs. 'I can understand that, I always hated it. I love baking, but cooking? Awful!'

Now I feel like leaning over to study her more closely. My mother-in-law, the staid housewife and mother, whose Sunday roast is the best I have ever had – *she* hates cooking?

'Glass of prosecco?'

'Yes, please!'

And so it goes on. It's not bad at all. We have a conversation that isn't totally boring, and I can see clearly now: only when I show myself as I really am and give her the chance to respond, only then can a real conversation develop. Everything else is fake.

We probably won't turn into besties, but whenever Granny comes visiting now, I am not stressed any more. I don't have to prepare anything; I can remain relaxed, because I no longer have to play-act. I don't even have to buy a cake. 'I brought something!' she trills, and she is happy, because my son loves her cakes. Me too.

Here now are a few more impressions about family life. Be inspired!

Presents and heirlooms

I have already mentioned the macramé thing ... Well, let's just say you can divide up presents into two groups. First there's:

- Perfect gifts that successfully meet the taste of the recipient
- Gifts you have especially asked for

Then there's the second group of presents:

- Presents that aim to meet the recipient's taste but don't quite hit it

- Practical things (which can cause tears and then a divorce if given by your partner)
- Presents the giver expects to be used by you
- Presents that the giver would like him/herself (a chainsaw, for example)

Depending on how big your attic or cellar is, you can of course keep everything you receive over the years. At best, you can remember who gave it to you and get it out when the giver comes to visit, like I did so often with the shitty macramé thing. Or you can just bin everything you don't want. Out with the junk!

Heirlooms are an advanced kind of present. They have not been chosen by you, nor by the giver; it is a case of sheer luck if you like the 48-piece dinner set or the fox fur stole. But one can only speculate how likely it is that your long-dead great-aunt on your mother's side and you have the same taste in crockery and fashion.

Heirlooms are difficult, because there are a whole bunch of emotions attached to every cup and saucer, and consequently one cannot simply reject them or take them straight to a charity shop. You can, of course, just not care about other people's feelings, but you would end up an arsehole, and that is not very nice – for you, or the people around you.

Another possibility is more practical: 'I don't have the space.' Say it while putting both hands to your cheeks, shaking your head and pretending to fight tears. 'The art deco vase from great-grandma! How beautiful! But I have nowhere to put it.' Or: 'The collection of porcelain figurines by the Charlesworth family! I wish I had space for it!' Shake head, hands on cheeks, fighting tears. There will always be a place for it, only not in your house.

That uncle is not allowed to come

This is one of the few cases when you can loudly state that you don't care without feeling bad. *That* uncle is not welcome, *basta*! He's the dick here, not you.

It doesn't matter what makes him so impossible. There are families at whose table an uncle is welcome who – and everybody knows it – has touched his niece indecently, or who has beaten up the aunt. And instead of being shown the door, he goes back to the buffet and gets himself another portion of potato salad.

That uncle of mine is a really unpleasant Nazi. I have no idea where he got it from, because all other members of my family are all right. *That* uncle, however, was always there, at every christening, confirmation and birthday – although there was one unspoken rule: he had to keep his mouth shut. Only when the younger generation, my cousin and me, told the family that we wouldn't go to future family gatherings if he was attending was he not invited any more. This was shortly after the wedding of said cousin when a more than generous helping of alcohol made *that* uncle forget to keep his mouth shut. The bridegroom's family originated in Nigeria. You can probably imagine what happened. Why he was tolerated for such a long time is due to a horrible feeling that thrives in families: guilt.

Don't give a damn about guilt!

Religion and politics

Apart from *that* uncle, there is, of course, a whole variety of other relatives with the most absurd opinions. Whether they are members of a foxhunt or a sectarian church, whether they are climate change deniers or conspiracy theorists – families are a colourful cross-section of God's big zoo. Other than with friends, you don't have to have endless discussions about respective quirks (particularly when it is about simply believing something or not.) Any discussion with family on these topics is usually useless anyway.

You can still meet those usual suspects for coffee and cake, of course, provided you are not tempted – as it is such a nice afternoon, and everything has been on such a rational level so far – to mention the hunting/sect/conspiracy/climate issue. Because it would be taken up with passion, particularly when a little brandy is on offer (see Auntie Mabel).

Some religiously motivated relatives (e.g., my Granny Glenda) possibly see it as their duty to remind their loved ones time and again of the only path towards heaven and being saved (even though she knows you have taken many an unfortunate shortcut, to stay with the metaphor). Does this count as annoying behaviour because it's about you? Hallelujah, yes! But what can you do if you don't want to keep wincing and hoping you can muddle through this kind of conversation with a few 'Hmms'? And what if, on your way home, you don't want to be angry about this kind of manipulative intervention (and you just want to go home calmly and bitch about Granny Glenda with L. instead)?

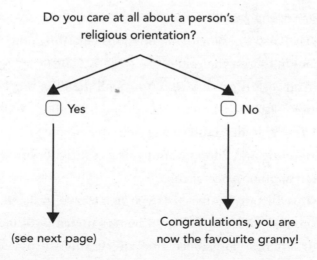

Do you care at all about a person's religious orientation?

☐ Yes

☐ No

(see next page)

Congratulations, you are now the favourite granny!

Think about it:

Try something like this: 'Yes, I can see what you mean, but I see that differently and I don't really want to discuss it now. Let's just tuck into this gorgeous cake instead. Do you want another piece?'

It is not necessary to remove Granny Glenda from your life, because we remember:

With friendliness you don't have to give a toss about all the topics that cause you to inwardly roll your eyes. Nobody will be cross with you if you publicly disagree about something (in case it is something you do happen to care about) as long as you keep being friendly.

Maybe Granny Glenda will actually have another piece of cake, and then her mouth will be full for a while, and you can change the subject.

That also works with her opinions regarding dogs. 'Dogs shouldn't sit on the sofa!'

And regarding children: 'You spoil the little one far too much!'

'Yes, I understand what you mean, but I see that differently and I don't want to discuss it right now. Do you want another piece of cake?'

Apart from the fact that you don't have to listen to all that crap (and that Granny Glenda's midriff will balloon) this strategy has a nice side effect: you are not shying away from saying what you think – and that feels really, really good.

Food

I like meat. For some people, this is a statement similar to saying 'I like eating babies.' There was a time when I didn't eat meat at all. Maybe I'll get there again, but since I had my baby, my very special diet mainly consists of his leftovers. We don't have a pig at home, and because I find it difficult to throw away food, I am that pig. My son simply loves sausages, salami and chicken legs, so my diet is the direct opposite of meatless.

I'm easy about this, but I seem to be the only person from far and wide not to see this issue emotionally. All my friends find the subject of diets hugely interesting, but it makes me yawn, and I simply stuff another roast beef sandwich into my gob. All those latest research results about broken-up proteins, left-turning radicals or all the bad things caused by white flour – well, I simply don't care. I have no opinion about the paleo diet or the ovo-lacto one – I'm simply not interested.

Other people can go on about it until the cows come home: L., for example, who loves talking about his low-carb diet, but not with me. I only have one specification for my food: it has to taste nice. Maybe you have different expectations, for example, that neither meat nor fish have a place on your plate or that is has to be kosher, halal or purple. Whatever, you have every right to expect this to be respected (but me too).

The reason I am bringing this up under the heading *Family* is that in my family, every gathering, whatever the occasion, is about food. You meet up to stuff yourselves. That makes sense because with many relatives one doesn't have much more in common than the fact that we need food to stay alive. This is also the reason any restriction in this area generally gets rejected. It is a risk to the common ground, i.e., the shared leg of lamb. The family peace is dependent on it.

In addition, the majority of people at family parties are older people who are not that open-minded about new food fads. They say: 'Why don't you eat blah blah blah? We have eaten blah blah blah all our lives and we have survived!' Followed by a joke about vegetarians – who always wear wellies because they are not allowed leather...?

Me, I can top that, because I eat everything, but only if I like it (at least a bit). I have stopped putting things into my mouth that I don't want just to keep peace with the cook or the baker. Do my relatives now think I am awkward? A princess lying on a pea? Touchy? I don't give a damn. As a result of being firm, I have saved myself from many a plateful of heart stew, tripe and sweetbread.

Family traditions

As we all know, families are a minefield – and family traditions are particularly dangerous. The most sensitive trigger of them all? Christmas. What will we eat, when are we exchanging presents, what music will we play, church or no church? Those are the cornerstones. Then there are the more trivial flashpoints, such as who is decorating the tree and when? What songs will we sing? During the weeks of the run-up, there is a lot of tension in the air. When will Santa Claus actually appear, and in what shape? Who will make the Christmas cake? And, crucially, whose recipe will be used? These details from the Grand Christmas Programme are at least as important as the actual feast.

In my family, for example, there is a tradition that butter cookies (a special recipe) are decorated with colourful icing. We always have light blue, pink, yellow and greenish biscuits. To change this is not possible for me. I wouldn't recognise the biscuits as Christmas biscuits. Along those lines, everybody has his or her own list of non-negotiables. My list is:

- Colourful biscuits
- Nice clothes
- Red Christmas baubles and straw stars to decorate the tree

Until last Christmas, there was another item on the list too:

- Fondue

Meaning meat fondue, because at home we always had beef fondue on Christmas Eve. Even during my meatless years, I made an exception at Christmas. I was a Christmas carnivore. Then I had the baby. His first Christmas was easy, because no matter how excited we were, he slept right through it. But there were stressful moments nonetheless, particularly because of this stupid thing under the fondue pot where you put the methylated spirit – the little burner. There were two reasons we didn't have fondue that year:

1. The thing had disappeared
2. There was no meth either

It is only due to the holiness of the day that we didn't end up in an almighty row about who is responsible for the storage of the kitchen gadgets. (It's L.)

The following year our son was wide awake and helped with the preparations, but he only has a limited attention span. That resulted in light blue, pink, yellow and greenish child's and dog's hair when we were baking. The tree also looked different to previous years. At the lower branches, up to about a metre high, my son hung up everything that he considered would make a nice Christmas decoration: socks, soft toys, aluminium foil and, to the dog's delight, slices of salami. Everybody was happy and content (particularly the dog). And then came Christmas Eve.

From midday onwards, L. was in the kitchen preparing the sauces to go with the fondue. That was great, and his sauces are really very good. He always makes five to six different ones, so he was busy all afternoon. That meant I never got around to dressing up myself or our son, or to wrapping up the last presents. 'Silent Night' also loses some of its festive effect when you are shouting: 'Don't lick the dog!', 'You shouldn't lick the dog!', 'I won't say it again!' every two minutes.

When the damned sauces were ready, we sat down to the fondue. L. was still wearing his apron, me my jogging bottoms, our boy used the fondue fork to stab his slippers, and we moved the fondue pot so far out of reach, so he wouldn't hurt himself with the hot oil and the flames, that we repeatedly had to get up to put the meat in and get it out again. Our son shrieked like a banshee, because that was exactly what *he* wanted to do. Then the flame under the pot went out. L. and I looked at each other in despair. Not again!

We did what we could. L. lifted the pot with the hot oil, I tried to fix the burner, and our son fed the dog with egg sauce, but in vain: the burner had given up the ghost.

But this year L. was well prepared. 'I have bought more meth, just in case!' he announced. Triumphantly he filled the burner up (he had even bought a replacement burner), but what can I say, the meth simply didn't light. Not at all. *Null, nada, niente.* You could have used this meth in a fire extinguisher. Eventually we cooked the best of Galician beef over a few tea lights to a light shade of grey and drowned it in sauces (apart from the egg sauce that had gone to the dog). But this too didn't last long, because the whole sorry episode had taken so long that the toddler didn't want to sit down any more, and I had to ring the little Christmas bell for him and turn the music back on. In short, it wasn't very Christmassy, at least not this part.

'Don't give a toss about the fondue,' we have said ever since. Well, not completely. This year we are having fondue on Christmas Day, quite relaxed, in jogging bottoms, one sauce fewer and our son is allowed to play or sit at the table, as he prefers. Nobody is going to care if the music is right, ring the little bell or notice whether the presents are in the right place. On Christmas Eve we are planning to have potato salad and frankfurters. That might turn into a new family tradition. As long as nobody changes it again, anyway.

Disappointing the parents

'No, we won't be going to Aunty Mimi's forty-seventh wedding anniversary.' 'No, we won't invite your neighbours to our wedding.' 'No, there won't be a second grandchild who might be a girl.' 'No, L. will not take over his father's business.' But most of all: 'No, under no circumstances will we go on a fortnight's cruise with the whole family.' In addition, I am not going to change into being 'something more serious', or do public readings wearing black-rimmed glasses, and I won't do my PhD either.

In these ways and others, I continuously disappoint

some family members, most of all my mother, who then does this slightly pained look and begins to hum.

The reason parents often have very high expectations of us is that from our birth onwards they think we are extra special. I am not immune to that and am convinced of the unique intelligence of my two-year-old. Even though he is still in nappies and really believes his granddad could steal his nose by putting his thumb between index and middle finger – it doesn't change my conviction that everything he does betrays an exceptional intelligence. This conviction will remain throughout childhood. Until adolescence.

During adolescence we start to disappoint our family. It starts with the clothes (depending on the era, it will be torn jeans, ultra-short skirts or baggy trousers), continues with the hairdo (long, shaved off or colourful) and ends with substances (cigarettes, alcohol, weed and more). It often ends with a big bang such as being expelled from school. Adolescence really should toughen up parents towards disappointments. But far from it!

You can normally split parental disappointment into two groups:

1. Profession/job
2. Choice of partner

According to our parents, particularly our mothers, we are batting well below our potential in both those areas. Mothers invariably think we all are unrecognised geniuses and very beautiful. Regarding partners, parents hold back very cleverly at first and only afterwards come clean: 'I knew from the beginning that he/she was not right for you!'

Regarding jobs, however, most parents don't hold back at all. Mine were – for whatever reason – utterly convinced that studying law would be exactly the right thing for me. I agreed, mostly, because I was clueless, and also because of the promised financial support. I swear I knew during the very first introductory talk about it that law was not for me. They talked and talked about traineeships and seminars and state exams, and after an hour and a half I came to the conclusion: *Yes, I now know some of the words.* In short, it was a disaster. But I didn't have an alternative. For several months I struggled with the knowledge that there would be a moment when I had to say to them: 'Hey, I'm quitting. Thank you for supporting me so far, but I've got a job in a pub now until I know what I want to do. Love you!' Were they disappointed? Of course they were! It is quite normal to disappoint your parents. If you don't, you would be a robot or a clone.

But it brought me great relief. Not only because I had finally said it, but also because **whenever we do what we need and want to do, we feel happy and free.**

Don't care about studying law or economics or whatever your parents want you to do. Choose your own path.

(It might help to remember that your own parents aren't Queen's counsels, judges at the High Court, astronauts, prime ministers or filthy rich. Unless, of course, they are Queen's counsels, judges at the High Court, astronauts, prime ministers or filthy rich.)

4

At Work

- Brainstorming
- Presents in the office
- It's all about you
- People pleasing
- After work
- Sacrificing
- Guilt
- Creating work for others

If you are able to deal with Auntie Mabel, *that* uncle and your parents' expectations, you would think that you could get on very well with your workmates and boss. Far from it! A day in the office is another minefield of difficult people and stressful situations, and that deserves a whole new arsenal of strategies to help you to rise above it all.

Brainstorming

In that super-cool advertising agency I have mentioned before, one of the things I'm planning not to bother with any more is brainstorming sessions. Have you ever done one? Brainstorming – literally, a storm in the brain – is supposed to create new ideas for a certain task by thinking about it in a group (in one recent memorable brainstorm at work, we had to come up with an advertising concept for a stoma, an artificial body opening). But a good deal of these brainstorms are mere brain farts. They stir the air, but not by much.

There are various methods for brainstorms that are supposed to stimulate creativity. One popular method is the one with the six hats. It was developed by Edward de Bono (who was probably totally pissed when he devised it). The participants take on particular roles, marked by different coloured hats. The white hat, for example, is for analytical thinking, the yellow hat is for the optimist, the black one is for the doubter, the red one is for feelings and intuition. The green hat is worn by the creative mind of the group, and the person with the blue hat runs the session. During the brainstorming the participants repeatedly swap hats and change roles. This forces you to take a different perspective, meaning you are less likely to block yourself and you will override your inner resistance.

Can you imagine it? Here are six grown-ups on office

chairs around a table – the men with full facial hair and suits, the women with manicured nails – and all have a colourful hat on as they try to say really clever things about an artificial anus. It is one of the situations when you imagine what this looks like from the outside and you just think: 'What on earth ...!'

'Stoma – because you're worth it!' is one of the first brain farts in the office with the glass walls. And for all the love in the world, it's enough for me.

'Is the brainstorming over already?' Eva asks me when, back in my office, I slump on the chair.

'No.' I shake my head, and the hat falls off. She looks at me dumbfounded. 'Have you ... did you simply run out?'

That's what it looks like.

Sometimes you do something instinctively and spontaneously and only explore later whether it was the best decision. The decision to leave the stoma brainstorming session, hat and all, was one of them. The reason was not the product, but the meeting itself, and it doesn't matter whether it is a meeting with or without hats. In no meeting I have ever attended until my bum went numb has my participation been in any way helpful. The main reason for this is that I am easily distracted by other people. I ponder whether Larissa has new hair extensions or not (she has), what it says on Brian's T-shirt (*advertfreak*) or whether those are dark sweat stains on Andrew's shirt. All this captures my attention much more than the subject of the meeting. In video conferences I try to make out objects in the background, and if one of the participants has a tic or a wart on their upper lip which moves when they speak, or if he or she says 'OK' after every sentence – I am lost. I am lucky after such a meeting if I remember what it was about. The notes I take during meetings generally consist of geometric patterns and cats lying down (I'm quite good at them). My son has, due to the strange notes I take at work, a very peculiar idea of what I do.

In short, meetings and teamwork are not for me. I am made for solitary ponderings in front of the laptop and, if possible, behind closed doors. The only person who doesn't get in my way is Eva. I have been sharing an office with her for such a long time that I know her every quirk, every idiosyncrasy and every outfit. She is part of my office. Others have cactuses on the windowsill – I have Eva. She is my office plant. And I really like her (now).

It is she who, after my escape from the brainstorming, says aloud what I had secretly feared: 'Won't Brian be cross with you?' Brian, the *advertfreak*, is my boss.

'Brian?' I warily peep through the door into his office. He is sitting behind his desk, staring at his oversized computer screen. 'Today at the meeting ...' I try, and in my mind I desperately search for alternative words for 'silly hats' and 'unbearable'.

'Yes, what is it?' Brian asks, not unfriendly, and looks at me.

'It's just that ... er ... the meetings ... er ... I'd prefer not to take part. I am much more effective on my own, and I could have a look at the—'

'OK!' says Brian and looks again at the screen. 'Can you believe it, United losing against this third-class team!'

'That was all?' Eva asks incredulously. We are sitting on our office chairs, staring at each other.

'Yes. He also said that only results counted and not the method of achieving them.' Sounds sensible. I am not sure why I am so surprised that Brian said something so rational. Of course, only results count for him, and nobody gains when I attend meetings, as I am as productive and efficient as the fruit bowl.

Why on earth haven't I said something before? I could have saved myself hours, days, probably weeks of meetings in hats! Somehow, I was always vaguely afraid to say it. But seriously, what could have happened? In the worst-case scenario Brian would have said, 'I don't care whether you like the meetings or not, you will attend!' What was I so anxious about?

When I tell L. in the evening, he looks at me with amazement. 'United lost?!'

Sometimes I could strangle him.

The thing with the meetings and the hats was an instinctive decision and not a conscious one, but it put me in such a good mood that I felt like singing 'We ... are ... the champions ...' every time I entered the office. I can do anything, if I want to, I am five inches taller than before, and nothing and no one can stop me now. But then ... there's Michelle.

Presents in the office

I guess there is a Michelle in every office. Our Michelle is petite, eager and presumably always used to sit in the front row in class at school. Michelle is not unlikeable and not a bad person or anything like that, but we don't have anything in common. Once in the back row, always in the back row. With the same eagerness Michelle always did blackboard duty, she is now busy recording and remembering all the birthdays of all her colleagues in the office on an Excel spreadsheet. A week before each date she throws herself into action. At first, she roams the rooms with a piggy bank she bought especially for this purpose and asks everyone for a donation. She also looks in the toilets in case someone is hiding there. A few days later she does the same round, but with a large card you are supposed to write something 'funny' in – though, in most cases something 'funny' is already printed on the front, such as: 'I AM 18 AND HAVE 35 YEARS OF EXPERIENCE'.

Hilarious, isn't it? On the actual birthday the respective person gets this on his/her desk, together with a present. It is invariably something of particular ugliness; I really have no idea where Michelle manages to find these things.

Blow-up cakes, fluffy unicorn slippers, and a plastic pistol Sellotape dispenser. We've had it all.

But Michelle is not only hyperactive around birthdays. She also makes her rounds when Alice's youngest starts school, the caretaker retires, Pia is leaving, or Augustus is in hospital because he broke a leg while skiing off-piste. The idiot. Rolling through our office is an endless loop of presents and cards for new job/old job/illness/getting better/Christmas. I once had a nightmare in which I had a fatal accident, but the worst thing was not the fact that I had kicked the bucket but that the whole office turned up at my funeral and Michelle had ordered the wreath.

It's not that I always reject the birthday celebrations of my workmates. My dear friend Eva's birthday is on 5 March, and she will get a home-baked hazelnut cream cake from me, because she likes it. The difference is that in this case (Eva, hazelnut cake), both parties (Eva, me) are happy. In the other cases (colleagues, fluffy unicorn slippers) nobody is happy – apart from Michelle.

For these reasons and, I admit it, my fear of unicorn slippers, I have decided: I'm not going to get involved in donations in the office any more. They don't make me happy, I don't like being part of it, I'd rather not do it, ergo: ta-da! I will let it go. The only thing that keeps me from putting this plan into action is what Michelle might think of me when I tell her I don't want her to count me in any more, and what the others may think when my name is no longer on their birthday cards. I ponder and ponder, but always come to the same conclusion: really, I don't care. Does Sandra from accounts approve of my actions? It simply doesn't matter.

All this goes through my head during the two minutes that Michelle stands in front of me, saying: 'Colleague blah blah blah ... passed driving test blah blah blah ... something funny blah blah blah.' And then she holds the piggy bank under my nose.

It is amazing that something that you really want to say, and which you are totally convinced is the right thing to say, is still so difficult to utter out loud:

'Michelle, I'm not going to take part in this any more, this donating. It is ... er ...' And only now do I realise that I should have prepared a clear and sound reason. 'It is about principles,' I say with a smile, while my brain goes bananas and inside my head I am parroting 'about *principles* ...?'

But it works. Michelle is slightly irritated but accepts it immediately. 'Oh, yes, well ... Yes, of course ... bye ...' And she takes herself away. As if I had disclosed to her that my religious convictions were against piggy banks and greeting cards.

'Maybe she thinks you have gone mad?' Eva ponders when I tell her, and the best thing is my honest response: 'I wouldn't give a toss if she does.'

The next time, after our conversation about principles, when Michelle is making her rounds with the piggy bank, I bump into her in the kitchen. Two workmates from the graphics department are standing next to me by the coffee machine, and when Michelle has relieved them of their cash and says 'Hello' to me and walks on, the two blokes look at me sideways. There is no outrage in their eyes, no disapproval, not even amazement. It is pure envy!

No more meetings, no fluffy unicorn slippers – these are mega results in terms of 'not giving a toss'. The best thing about not giving a shit any more is that it makes you feel like Wonder Woman. There is a slight niggling bad conscience regarding the driving test, the anniversary, the good-bye to the intern, but then – *Olé!* – you can let it go. It doesn't help anybody. *We are the champions, my friend ...*

It's all about me!

Our stoma client taught me an important lesson. He turns up after a week, as expected, to have a look at all the creative ideas the team has come up with regarding artificial body openings. For occasions like this, the client is shown to our most beautiful meeting room and pampered with coffee, chocolates, a fruit bowl and lots of bright optimism. Two concepts have been accepted for further consideration. One of them is mine, and (unfortunately) I will have to present it myself.

There are people, I believe, who flourish in such a situation. I am not one of them – surprise, surprise. I always have to make a great effort not to mumble, I keep staring at my notes, and as soon as someone coughs, I lose the thread of what I'm saying. My hands are already sweaty, even though it isn't my turn yet (I am on second). I cast a quick sideways look at the client. He looks friendly, his smile is benevolent, and every now and then he nods. He seems to like the idea he's being presented and there is a positive mood in the room. All is good. Then it is my turn.

When I step in front of the large blackboard (this is so totally *vintage* and therefore *cool*) and start to present my concept, I see how the client is starting to pull a face. His brow is wrinkled like a thunder cloud, the corners of his mouth are turning down, and then he folds his arms.

You don't have to be an FBI personality profiler to read the whole of his body language as a big fat disapproval. Damn! I had been so sure about my ideas, but what this client is communicating to me without saying a word is: 'That is the stupidest thing I have ever come across.'

I hurry to end the presentation, because I do not want to prolong the suffering unnecessarily. At the end I take my laptop and my notes, and while everybody gets up for a stretch, the client claps – once.

'Fine!' he says. 'Thank you very much.'

In my mind I add: 'And what the hell was that performance of the little brunette all about?'

But then he continues: 'I think we are well on our way with the second concept.' And he invites Brian and me for lunch.

Eh...? What is happening here? I think I can tell you now.

Between tiramisu and a grappa, I found out that the client has an ingrown toenail. Very trivial, and very painful. While at the beginning of our meeting everything was fine in his shoe, the pain began during my presentation. It became increasingly unbearable because his shoes were too tight. Nonverbally he had communicated: 'That is the stupidest thing I have ever heard!' but what he really meant was: 'Ouch, dammit, this fucking toenail!' Those are two totally different statements.

I always think of him now whenever I feel unsure about someone else's reaction. When, for example, Brian or the bus driver or the baker greets me in a grumpy way, it often doesn't have anything to do with me. Maybe they have an ingrown toenail, or United have lost – again. Whatever it is, I won't guess any more, because I remember to let it go and not care about the grumpy people. Thanks to an ingrown toenail!

On closer examination, my office days are brimming with potential opportunities to not give a damn. Let's have a look at another few:

People pleasing

People pleasing is a very big thing in the office world. Whether it is about doing overtime, swapping holiday dates or for someone to just *quickly* have a look at some computer problem, there are people who always say, 'Yes, of course.' Even though they are really thinking: '*For God's sake, I'd rather hack my right arm off!*'

I am one of those people. I have done my colleagues so many favours that I hardly know what to do with all my Brownie points. God knows why. Apparently, us yay-sayers are afraid that people won't like us any more when we say no to their requests. We want to *please*. Maybe. What confirms this theory is that when it comes to people I know very well, of whose positive feelings towards me I am sure, I don't find it at all difficult to say no. L. knows that.

My brain of course realises that one 'no' doesn't make people dislike me. I don't have to suffer in order to be liked. I know also that someone with clear boundaries is treated with more respect, but as soon I am in a situation like that, my brain fails. I find it extremely *awkward*, and I alleviate the situation by simply saying 'Yes, of course' – and afterwards kick myself hard, because I have failed again.

There is one person in the office who is responsible for my particularly high score of Brownie points: Mark. His sentences frequently start like this:

- Could you just ...?
- I have a problem here ...
- Have you got a minute ...?
- There's another thing ...

And before you know it, I am dealing with a problem that isn't mine. At least, not originally – though of course now it is. Does it annoy me? Oh, yes. Does it affect me personally? Absolutely. That is why from now on my guideline is: sod people pleasing (and Mark). It doesn't mean that I will never, ever help Mark out, but it will no longer be my customary reaction.

'What shall I say then?' I ask Jana in the Pimpernel over a Martini.

'How about "no"?' Jana suggests.

I look deep into her eyes. 'You are not a big help, my darling!'

The best expert advice for spineless idiots like me is to ask for some time to think about it.

'Could you quickly look at this text for me please?'

'I'll let you know in ten minutes.'

What a super solution. The only problem is that ten minutes later I will again have to say no and face the same music.

Another suggestion is to pay a compliment to the other person before you deny the request.

'Could you quickly go over this text please?'

'Oh, I love checking your texts, but this time, sorry, I can't.'

That sounds much better than a simple no.

The next morning, I turn up in the office all excited. I am expecting a practice run. And I get it at the end of the day in the shape of Mark who predictably darkens my door when I have just shut down my laptop.

'Hey, Alex, finished already?'

'Yes.' Now ... now it's happening, I am thinking, and my heart beats a bit faster.

'Could you quickly look at my text please? There seems to be something missing.'

OK, this is the moment!

'Mark, I love looking at your texts, but at the moment I can't.'

And I smile my brightest smile. But why don't I feel relieved that I have finally made the leap? A second later I know why. Mark doesn't accept my 'no'. My unconscious has probably registered this long before the rest of my brain, that's why I hadn't relaxed. Mark keeps darkening my door. Maybe something about me has given him a signal that there is room for negotiation.

'But I need to send it off this afternoon, come on, it won't take long ... please, *please!*' He cocks his head and gives me a big smile.

It's a situation for professionals, I think. How does he dare to make his problem with the deadline my problem?

It's outrageous! Mark has a history of letting things build up and then, at the last minute, asking everyone else for help. It's not true that it won't take long. If I start now, it'll be at least one or two hours before I finish. *He doesn't take me seriously!* I think, and there is little ball of anger rising in my belly. It reminds of when I finished my friendship with Catherine. At that moment I was able to harness my anger to overcome my sense of wanting to please. I resolved to do the same now. It's not exactly a mindfulness method, but it works. I think: I have been in this office for eight hours, and Mark has the nerve to try to dump this shit on me. Automatically I sit more upright and straight. Anger needs more space than empathy. And then there's the idiotic grin he has on his face! Does he really think he can persuade me with his puppy-dog eyes? How stupid does he think I am? Well, I have to concede, it's been successful quite a few times in the past.

I cock my head like he does and look him straight in the eye. Mark's charming smile freezes somewhat. 'No, thank you,' I say, and this time he gets it. And then, finally, from deep within me, there is a sense of triumph rising to the surface and flooding me, at the same time driving away the anger. In my best mood I grab my handbag and give the gobsmacked Mark a pat on the shoulder.

Mark is not mad at me, by the way. He doesn't hate me, he doesn't think I am selfish nor does he spread a rumour in the office that I smell. Quite the opposite: I have the impression that he generally takes everything I say and do a bit more seriously. If there is a problem, I will help if I can, but, of course, only if I want to. And I'm getting better at it. When Lena asks me whether I could write a report about her internship for her, I don't hesitate a second. 'I'd rather hack off my right arm,' I answer. Then we have a laugh together, and the request is forgotten.

After-work dos

If you consider it a real achievement to get through office hours without having strangled colleagues or your boss, events after work are clearly an absurd idea. I mean, whoever had this screwball notion? Has anyone ever looked around after an eight-to-ten-hour day in the office and said: 'Oh, I really would like to see some more of you all; let's spend another few hours together!' Is that even technically possible? What unfortunate twist of fate has led us to a situation where the phrase 'after-work event' is taken to mean anything other than simply something that happens after work, *which has nothing to do with work.*

I can tell you about a few things that I like doing after work: I like to go home, cook, go for a drink, drive through the park, have an ice cream, play with my son. There are approximately a million things that I like doing after work. The list includes some absurd things like driving a tractor, trying out a wind tunnel and tickling carp, but never, never, never will my list feature 'sit with a giggling Michelle and a pissed Mark in the Gin Bar around the corner from the office'. I am so sure about this because I have done it once or twice.

When I had just started at the agency, a new fad of 'after-work parties' took hold. It was like going clubbing, only at half past six in the afternoon instead of at eleven, and with snacks. It was devised for people in cool offices like consulting, advertising and media who:

1. Had no family waiting with dinner.
2. Didn't have to go to bed early because the next day was just another cool workday.

Various employers then came up with the brilliant idea that it would be very efficient if team members had after-work snacks together. Dainty little sandwiches would improve the interdisciplinary communication and the employees could talk with each other and exchange information about work problems and tasks. The best thing about it: it didn't waste precious work time!

Brian suggested many such meetings, primarily with the aim to make the team bond. The effect was the opposite. Some people were annoyed that they were asked to stay late, others felt obliged to attend, even though they had a family waiting at home. Some didn't want to go and were in a bad mood (me) or didn't like the location. The meetings were boring and everyone looked at a bit of a loose end and didn't know what to do – apart from eating sandwiches. I assumed this whole after-work agenda would quickly disappear without a trace, but then something happened.

Ironically, it was Brian who did something that really bonded the work team, albeit involuntarily: he took on a new manager. This new manager behaved so unbelievably lousily towards everybody that their hatred of him welded the team together like nothing else. There is an old Chinese proverb that turned out to be very true indeed:

The happiness of a village
Depends on one person everybody hates.

From then on, some colleagues met after work in the Gin Bar as often as humanly possible to let off steam and to bitch about the manager. I was an enthusiastic and energetic member of this group and ranted like nobody else. As a newcomer, it made me feel fully integrated in the team. But after a time, it ran out of steam. The aforementioned manager changed his behaviour, and in addition, I found it increasingly absurd that I was not only annoyed about him during office hours, but also afterwards. I wasn't even paid for it! This wonderful insight came to me during a drink after work, and all at once I looked around and came to the conclusion: we had nothing in common with each other, apart from our anger. Not including Michelle and Mark, who after the second gin moved closer together. But then I was leaving already.

The hardcore group has remained faithful to the Gin Bar and meet up every Friday night for drinks. It has become quite a routine for them. That is nice, and Michelle and Mark (M&M) have got together, but I don't want to be part of it. I don't want to talk about work after work and rant about colleagues. I want to go home, take my bra off and be with my loved ones.

And exactly that – apart from the bit with the bra – I will now say aloud, because so far, I have thought of an excuse every Friday afternoon, hoping that one day they won't ask me again. Far from it.

'It's Friday today, you know what that means,' says Sandra from accounts first thing that morning.

'That tomorrow is Saturday?' I try with a wink, but it doesn't work.

'It's gin day. Are you coming?'

I take a deep breath and simply say it. That I won't come. Not today and not on any other Friday in the future, because after work I prefer to go home. Also, I don't particularly like gin. My sentences are still a little clumsy, but after the next person asks (Dennis from IT) it gets better. At the end of the day, when one of the trainees asks me the same question, I have progressed to: 'Nope. Not for a million dollars! But have fun!' Life can be so easy.

Sacrifices

It is a bit like believing in the Easter Rabbit or Santa Claus: the assumption that if only you slave away enough the boss will notice it and someday reward you for it. It is a common misconception with the result that armies of employees take on tasks they don't want, they are not responsible for and for which they are overqualified. If the boss is an arsehole, he will cleverly exploit this common fallacy.

When I met Jana, I was working freelance as a contractor in a production company, which meant I was obliged to put in as many hours as an employee, but without a fixed salary, no holiday pay and no national insurance. Jana was on an internship in the same company meaning she worked full-time without any money. Our boss, the owner of the company, loved this way of running a business. She also succeeded in making us not only grateful and happy to be allowed to work for her, but also feel bad when occasionally we didn't volunteer for overtime. But as there was so much to do, what would she do without us? She was a manipulative bitch.

We had an inkling that it wasn't quite right, but it took us a year and a half until we quit and pissed on the generous hourly rate of £ 1.25. It happens. Sometimes you end up with a boss who is not fair, not helpful or not a good person. Who is a dick.

Or Brian. He is a boss who is lovely, but extremely

forgetful. 'You could help out with a presentation for once!' he'll say.

And when I counter: 'But I have prepared the last ten presentations all by myself!', Brian says: 'Really?'

Even if I did a hundred presentations, he wouldn't notice. Workloads never get balanced out. Therefore, it doesn't make sense to do the extra work time and again.

Guilt

Guilt is another issue at work, including towards colleagues. You can develop your own feelings of guilt, but they sometimes get put on you by others.

A champion of this was one of the pub landlords I worked for during uni. It was quite normal in that pub to swap shifts or come in when someone was ill, that was no problem. The problem was that we were permanently understaffed, and it was a disaster when even one person didn't turn up. I had already postponed one exam to the next term in order to serve students beer and peanuts rather than revise. But then I had to put on the brakes.

'I can't do so many extra shifts any more,' I said very clearly.

The pub owner replied: 'But then your colleagues will have to work even *more*! Think of Sonya!'

Technically he was right. Without me, the others would have to work more, and it was also true that Sonya was a single mother who shouldn't have to do this. But there was also the fact that he should simply have taken on more people, and he didn't want to do that. Instead he made it my problem, and to convince me, he gave me some nice, fat feelings of guilt.

Only when he lost his driving licence and told me I was also supposed to do the shopping at the wholesaler did I rip off my apron and throw it at his feet. In his opinion, it was all *my* fault that he would now have to shut down the pub and we all would lose our jobs, not his, even though he had lost his licence because he was pissed and had dropped off in the car at a traffic light. The police had woken him up.

Do you recognise the strategy? If you do, repeat after me: I don't care anymore about feelings of guilt.

Creating work for others

There is another common situation where you might feel guilty at work: when your company takes on trainees who have to do as you say. They usually get paid normally (other than Jana; see above), and therefore they are mostly in a very good mood and really lovely. And that is the problem. They are so nice that you don't want to give them any work.

At first, I didn't really notice I was doing this, but then, one day, I was standing by the photocopier next to two trainees and they looked at me as if I was crazy. Instead of sending 'my' trainee Lena to do the photocopying, I didn't want to bother her so I was doing it myself – while Lena was surfing the net.

Since then I have watched out for it and have caught myself doing the following things:

- I have tidied up her projects myself rather than giving them back to her and asking her to do them again.
- I have let her go on time even when there was more work to do, which I then did myself.
- I have tidied up her desk at the end of the day before I went home.
- I have done some shopping for her in the lunch break.

'I'd like to be your trainee,' L. grins when I tell him about my observations.

'Ty-nees,' says my son happily. All three of us are tidying up the living room – as we do every night when the boy has spread his toys over the space like a juicer without the lid on.

'You have to help us. Why don't you put the Lego into the box?' I try to encourage him, and it works to a degree. 'And now let's take the soft toys to bed,' I continue, and in the end, he is beaming with pride.

'Done!' What a darling!

And then the darling takes his shoes off. For the first time. 'Wow!' I marvel. 'When did he learn that?'

L. is smiling. 'He has been practising for a few days.'

Squealing happily, our son gives me his shoe. The last few days it was L. who picked him up from nursery and got him dressed and undressed, and he gave him the time to do most things by himself, unlike me. It's true. When the little one starts to fumble around with something I take over far too quickly. Like with my trainees.

This insight is still with me the next day. Trainee Lena is a bit older than my son and can express herself more clearly, but secretly I now make use of my new knowledge to create work for her – without feeling guilty. I make her redo things, send her to do the photocopying and pick up my dry-cleaning during lunch. If I didn't know that I was secretly imagining she was a child, I would say: I am born to be a boss!

There are a million and a half stumbling blocks at work. Please check the list yourself:

- I don't want to make a fuss/delegate work to others.
  Yes / No
- I feel I have to make myself indispensable, so I don't get sacked.
  Yes / No
- I don't dare say no.
  Yes / No

- I would like my colleagues/boss to like me.

    Yes / No
- I do things I don't want to do in the hope it will be rewarded someday.

    Yes / No
- I take on tasks for which I am overqualified.

    Yes / No

And then – *Olé!*

5

Parents and Children

- Advice
- Taste
- Rules
- Plans
- Other parents
- Trying to make childless people understand

Pregnancy is the time when you don't have to give a toss about many things. Simply saying 'I don't feel like it' is an acceptable excuse. For everything.

It is a nine-month crash course in all the things you don't want to give a shit about any more. Technically, it wouldn't be possible any other way. If you didn't dismiss 90 per cent of all comments, advice and reactions, you would simply explode.

While your neighbour gushes about her totally natural birth in her bath, your mother-in-law tells you that a home birth would be the equivalent of wanting a stillbirth. Oh, you'll have to get rid of the dog now too, by the way, even though another friend declares that the dog can stay, but blankets in a cot are too high risk.

They all supposedly back up their advice by telling you of things they have heard at some time, but they all seem to stem from a horror movie. And while you are still reeling from seeing the second line appear on the pregnancy test, the potential grannies and granddads are already arguing whether your as-yet-unborn child will go to university or not.

Not many people know that the 'blissful' smile of pregnant women, which everybody mentions, is simply a *smile-and-nod* reaction towards all well-meaning advice givers. It is a kind of 'fuck everything' response, the only way not to freak out.

It is a wonderful gift of nature that you don't have to consider the advantages and disadvantages of this reaction, nor make a decision, nor do anything rational to achieve this attitude: it simply happens.

Relatively quickly you get to the point where you immediately grab some of those delicious cheesy snacks while other people are still in a hot debate about which sausages and what cheeses are allowed during pregnancy.

A pregnancy is particularly handy for people who find it difficult to put their own needs first and always try to get things right for everybody else. The fact that the baby has automatically assumed number one position means the rest of the world has been pushed pretty far down the line. For many people it is a completely new experience.

It's suddenly easy not to care that a whole row in the cinema has to get up for you, twice, because you need to go to the loo. Someone else is much more important than those other people, and that someone is jumping up and down on your bladder.

Advice

The unpleasant thing about advice during pregnancy is that parents-to-be only want the best for their baby and therefore have a tendency to be open to all kinds of nonsense. My ex-sister-in-law told me during my pregnancy not to eat pineapple, because it could cause a miscarriage. She said in some countries pineapples are actually used for terminations. Pineapples! I love pineapples! My midwife said I would have to eat half a ton of pineapples for anything to happen, but I didn't touch one for the whole time I was pregnant.

When I look back now to those nine months, only two pieces of advice were useful, both from my friend Josh:

1. Don't listen to advice!
2. Don't watch *Alien* after the second trimester.

The second piece of advice I understood because I *had* watched *Alien* and couldn't feel the first movements of my baby without some apprehension.

Here some pieces of advice that parents-to-be shouldn't give a toss about:

Everything about the development of the pregnancy

This nearly turned into the same kind of fiasco as the thing with the pineapple.

'Whoa! What month are you?' people would say. 'Your tummy is quite *big/small/low down/round*!'

If you hear this more than once, you become unsure of yourself. But don't take any notice. Don't give a toss. All questions about your weight gain will stop immediately if you ask the other person the same.

Everything about sleep

The advice goes like this: *Sleep a lot now, because once the baby has arrived, you won't have time for that!*

I mean, what is the point of that? Is there really some-one out there who believes that you should take to your bed now and sleep, because in two months' time you won't get any? If that were so, I could dance the night away now, because twenty years ago I stayed in bed for a whole week.

Everything regarding names

To give the baby a suitable and lovely name, parents

consult many books and hundreds of websites and have numerous discussions. You look for a name that is timeless and classic but not too sophisticated; that is short and sweet but not stupid; one that sounds good with your surname and the child's middle name; one that isn't too common but not too exotic either. Then you look at the list of choices and realise how many of those names are already taken by people you don't like. They get eliminated. Along with the names already taken by other relatives, friends or pets. If you are very lucky and there is a name left, there is a good chance your partner doesn't like it at all. And then, once you have finally found a compromise, there is at least one friend who will say: 'Hmm ... I don't know ... I think the name somehow sounds old-fashioned/stupid/boring/like a pet's name.'

And you start again.

Everything regarding the birth

Seeing a pregnant tummy, lots of women immediately get the urge to talk about their own experience of giving birth. As a rule, the labour was very painful, there were lots of complications, and it lasted about a million hours. These reports are like penis comparisons. Stop listening, if possible, and don't give a toss. Your baby's birth will be completely different.

... And everything else

Advice from loved ones (and not so loved ones) at least doesn't lack humour. A little survey among my friends and acquaintances turned up the following nonsense:

- When Katie was eight months pregnant her mother said: 'You don't have to buy anything for the baby yet. Just in case something happens. Your husband can buy it all when you are in hospital.'
- Laura heard from her mother-in-law: 'Two weeks after the birth you can go on a weekend trip with your husband. The baby can stay with me. Don't turn into a mother hen.'
- Nelly was told by a neighbour: 'If you have an epidural you will have headaches and a bad back for months and can never give your baby a bath.'
- Rita was told by her aunt: 'God, you drink two to three litres of water a day? Don't! The baby might drown.'

Please add to the list all the ridiculous things you have heard, and maybe add people whose opinion you won't give a damn about during pregnancy to the list too:

- ....
- ....
- ....

Taste

Buying baby things is wonderful. It is positive anticipation expressed in pounds sterling. The little cot (for him/her to sleep in!), a dummy (for his/her comfort!) or the muslin cloths with the cute prints (for him/her to vomit on!) – they are amazing. It makes this very unreal, absurd idea of having a baby a bit more real.

Thanks to Pintcrest, I had a very clear idea of how the nursery and the furniture and the baby would look. Colour scheme, patterns, brands – everything was ready in my head. After studying all those pictures, I was also very clear that without curvy wooden block letters spelling his name above the cot, he would not be able to sleep. I also learned that motifs of little bears and rabbits are out for baby accessories and we now have foxes and owls. Another indispensable thing: bunting to be hung in one corner of the nursery. And while I was still contemplating the colour schemes of light grey-and-mustard or turquoise-and-yellow, the first parcels from the excited grandmothers started arriving. They contained items that had never been placed on Pinterest by anybody. They were the antithesis of everything I had ever liked.

As an example of this clash, we had a Winnie the Pooh in light blue and pink from my mother-in-law on the future baby-changing table opposite a grey-blue whale from me, staring at each other. Sometimes, when looking at them, I hum the tune of *The Good, the Bad and the Ugly*.

When we eventually discovered that the baby would be a boy, my mother-in-law was so kind as to offer to buy us the complete first kit: towels, sleeping suits, bodysuits, mittens, the lot. Only at the last minute could I negotiate a deal: we would buy the things together. On the arranged day I waddled with man and belly towards the shopping centre, humming the Toreador song from *Carmen*. I was prepared for a tough fight:

Mother-in-law: 'Here, look! Light blue fleecy bodysuits with teddy bears on!'

Me: 'Forget it. I want little joggers with owls on.'

Then, I imagined, we would have an argument and hit each other and pull each other's hair in the middle of Mothercare. And all the buggies and prams would fall over like dominoes. L. wouldn't be able to help, because he simply didn't understand the importance of owls vs. teddy bears.

When we actually arrived at the shop, Mother-in-law was already pawing the pavement, a large shopping trolley in front of her, ready to fill it come what may.

'I've seen such cute hats,' she beamed, taking my arm and pulling me towards them. The hats were ... so-so, but Mother-in-law had already discovered something else and pulled me on. A crocheted suit in light blue.

'*Sweeet!*' she trilled and held it in front of my face. It was awful. Not simply 'not so nice' but an actual nightmare in light blue. I had come with the firm decision to refuse everything that I didn't like. This was my first baby and would probably be my only one, so everything had to be perfect. In light-grey-and-mustard or turquoise-and-yellow.

Then something very strange happened.

When I saw my mother-in-law with the awful crochet creation, my resistance melted like snow in the sun. It is very difficult to disappoint someone who is practically glowing with enthusiasm. I had to smile, because there was so much happiness and enjoyment in her face. I felt all warm and fuzzy inside, because it was so visible how much she was looking forward to her grandson. She held the crocheted suit towards me.

'What do you think?' she asked. And I gave her a kiss.

'Perfect!' I said (and then smuggled a pair of little tracksuit bottoms with owls on into the trolley).

This story could contain many opportunities for not giving a toss. For example, you might choose to ignore your mother-in-law's opinion about everything. Sometimes, depending on the person, that is not the worst decision. You could get everything in turquoise and yellow and it would look fantastic, but I want to tell you something: whenever my son later wore the crochet combo in light blue, it made me smile, because I had such lovely memories of seeing all the love and anticipation in his granny's face. That never happened with the tracksuit bottoms with the owls.

Rules

Once the baby arrives, you can relax. You will do everything wrong, but you have a whole army of specialists by your side to tell you how to do it right: everybody who has children, and everybody who doesn't. They are extremely willing to give you advice, whatever the topic – but each of those topics is a minefield.

Breast or bottle? BANG! If you breastfeed, when do you stop? BANG! When and where will be baby sleep? BANG! Babysitters? BANG! Burping methods? BANG! Going back to work full-time? BANG! Vaccinations? DOUBLE BANG!

Everybody defends his or her view of the world, what they deem right, and there are about as many opinions as there are PEOPLE ON THIS PLANET.

The stupid thing is that you don't give a damn about any of it, but each of these issues is one the parents have to come to a decision about and find a compromise over. That is very intimidating. You cannot even rely on the latest in scientific research as a yardstick – the bestselling baby guide of the year 1934 advised mothers to 'tame' their 'tyrannical' babies by not giving them much attention or cuddles. The crying would strengthen their lungs, and for that reason a well-fed and dry baby could be left alone for the night without any problems. At that time, it was an advantage if a mother didn't take the official advice too seriously and instead listened to her gut feelings. To this day, my mother starts crying when she sees how I cuddle my baby – because when I was little she stopped herself from doing it and always missed it. It wasn't the done thing then, to 'spoil' babies like that. In short, it is not easy for young parents to form their own opinion about all this, but most of them try their best. And then people turn up from all corners and tell you they 'have read something', 'heard something', or 'know that ...'

To avoid your eyes dropping out from rolling too much, it helps to remember that they all mean well. Sometimes people simply don't know how to express their desire to help, their attention or their love. They aren't all know-it-alls and don't all lack trust in the capabilities of a young mother. A good way to keep unsolicited advice at bay is to divert their attention with a practical question. Ask something specific that you find a bit difficult: the baby has a blocked nose and can't sleep, it always cries when getting dressed, whatever. Maybe you will get some good advice.

My favourite response is still: 'Here, just hold him for a second.' Whoever has a baby on their lap immediately stops giving lectures and starts cooing instead. It's the nicest way possible of avoiding the problem!

But there is one group of people I have no pity for: people who keep saying: *'We didn't have it. You don't need it either.'*

What kind of argument is that? I don't understand it. The first time I heard that sentence I had just bought a nappy bin. It is a pedal bin with a lid, which prevents you smelling whether the baby has done a poo or not as soon as you enter the house. I think it's a very good invention.

But when Auntie Mabel came to visit, I heard it: 'We never had something so complicated, and we still coped.' I was speechless. How do you come up with such an argument?

If Auntie Mabel had been around when some clever clogs invented the wheel, she would have said:

- 'We don't have to be that quick. We never needed to be quick before.'
- 'Rolling! As if carrying was not good enough!'
- 'How are all the square things going to deal with it?'

I simply didn't get it. Shit smell in the air or no shit smell in the air? Do we really need to discuss this? The blueprint for my revenge came from Mabel herself, because she then told me about her hip operation. Mabel has a new hip. The old one crumbled away. When she told me the new joint was made from some double-tempered cobalt-chrome-something, the time came. I took a sip of coffee and said: 'What nonsense. We never had that, and we still coped.'

Did I offend Auntie Mabel? Maybe. But offended or not, I'm not prepared to listen to rubbish.

A few weeks ago, I met up with an old school friend. She is four months pregnant and had just bought an 'Angelsound'. That is an 'Ultrasound Foetal Doppler', a gadget with low ultrasound frequency you can use to listen to the baby's heartbeat at home. I went in with full force: 'Well, we didn't have that when I was pregnant, and we ...'

Plans

We will divide the chapter about 'plans' into two sub-categories:

1. Plans about the pregnancy and the baby
2. All other plans

Plans you can really and truly not give toss about are all the ones in Category 1 – as well as all the plans in Category 2.

Seriously, it doesn't work. Luckily, you gain this insight quite gradually, so it is never a big surprise when your offspring decides not to go to university but instead wants to work in the pub 'for another year or so'.

I have nothing against plans, Plans are great! I have always made all sorts of plans. When I was pregnant, I made even more. I planned and planned and planned. I planned to lie on a deckchair in the sun with my huge belly, drinking smoothies. I planned to work until a few days before the birth. I planned to kit out the nursery plus the first set of clothes entirely in light grey and mustard (see above). And then I made the biggest plan of all plans: the Birth Plan.

According to my Birth Plan, the birth was to take place

under water, without painkillers and with background music by Jack Johnson. I also planned our first outings with the pram. I imagined how beautiful and tidy our home would be when, for a few months, I would be just a housewife and mother. I saw myself with the pram in a street café and going shopping without time constraints. I would go to one of those 'mother and child' Pilates courses, and on a Sunday morning L. and I and the baby would have a lie-in and just fool around in bed. Ha. Ha. Ha.

It started during pregnancy. When my belly was big and round, there was no way I would have fitted into a deckchair. I feared I would never get out of it again on my own and, furthermore, this slightly backward-leaning position seemed to be a signal for the baby to dance around like a bunch of monkeys. I vomited my first (and last) smoothie with such force that to this day I haven't touched another one – this is also out of consideration for my downstairs neighbours, because it landed on their balcony.

It also wasn't possible to work right up till shortly before the birth because my brain had turned into a bowl of lukewarm porridge. I couldn't concentrate for five minutes. Strange things happened: after going shopping my purse ended up in the freezer, and I let the bottle of water simply drop from my hand after I had filled my glass. In short, I wasn't quite there mentally.

The biggest joke, however, was my Birth Plan. That is

a contradiction in itself. In hindsight, I haven't got the foggiest why hospitals offer you such a thing. Presumably, they just want to make a good impression. You simply cannot determine beforehand what will be good for you when you are actually at it. For me, for example, it felt really good to rant and rave at L. during labour. Nothing on earth would have got me into a birthing pool at that point. But you can't write that into a Birth Plan.

During the next stage, the one when you moan loudly, exactly like they do in films, I couldn't rant any more. And when it got even worse, I demanded painkillers. 'Oh, your plan says you don't want any medication, only a natural birth,' the young blonde midwife trilled, but then she ran off after I had threatened to kill her if she didn't immediately come up with some good stuff. The mere idea of listening to Jack Johnson's songs while my mind was counting down to the next time I exploded with pain – it's perfectly possible that the iPhone wouldn't have survived it.

This experience was only a sample of what happened with the other plans. None of them actually materialised. My planning had not taken certain issues into consideration, for example the lochia, the post-birth bleeding that caused me to lie in bed with thick pads on, instead of leisurely pushing the pram in the spring sun. 'Confinement' is the correct term for this phase.

Also, my plans had not accounted for something else: the baby. It turned out very quickly that the baby didn't like shopping and street cafés at all. I could only walk past them. My Sunday plans also turned out a bit differently. L. fooled around with the baby, but in the living room, so that mama could get a bit more sleep. And the state of my house, since I was 'only' a housewife and mother – let's not go there. Let other mothers make organic jam, sew baby clothes and decorate the house. I counted it a success if I simply managed to have a shower and get dressed each day. Not even the Pilates course happened. It always coincided with the baby's midday nap.

From this and a hundred other situations I have learned not to care about plans. Any plans. All the stress you create for yourself to make them happen – let it go. I finally do what Buddhists have always preached: I enjoy the moment and accept whatever comes my way.

Other parents

I am now an extremely enthusiastic mother. All the things everybody had warned me about – 'You will see, once the baby arrives ...' – such as not enough sleep or not much time for other things, don't bother me much. From the moment I managed to adjust to the baby's rhythms and routines, and, if necessary, sometimes stayed in bed for a couple of days, all went quite smoothly. But nobody had warned me of the immense impact a baby can have to throw you off course.

Your whole life changes – so they say. Now I know what they meant. It's not about getting less sleep or learning you can't spontaneously go on weekend trips any more, but rather something nobody can really communicate to you: that the birth of a child creates a soft spot in your heart that will make you very vulnerable forever. Your own life is suddenly not as important as your baby's and you will never not be with him – no matter where you are. You will never again read headlines about disasters without thinking: 'What if that was my child?' Another person's happiness is now more important than yours, and the worst thing in this short life is the time you are not spending with your baby. Your own heart is so much bigger. You never would have thought it before. And, of course, nobody tells you that you can go for several days without a shower.

This is all so amazing and overwhelming! But despite my huge enthusiasm for my child, there are some disadvantages. Other children's parents, for example.

In the beginning they just turn up in your life in the form of other pregnant women. If in your circle of friends nobody else is pregnant, you simply get to know other ones in your antenatal classes. It's like being back in school, thrown together with a bunch of people who would otherwise never spend time with each other. When I first attended my course, I looked automatically for the back row. But no, you sit in a circle. The other preggers chat about the hospitals they have visited, discuss birthing stools and various positions for giving birth. But I couldn't really get into this. I didn't like the tea that was on offer either.

It felt like being in a room of Michelles from work, but then it was also like being in school: you find like-minded people, or at least one person. In my case, she was sitting next to me and was also not particularly actively engaged in the discussions. I noticed her again when we had to lie down for the 'Fantasy Journey'. We were told to relax, while the midwife told us a story about a castle, and that a good fairy comes out and asks us for our wishes. And then I heard my neighbour. She had started to snore loudly.

That broke the ice. This woman was called Meena and she was really nice. I could chat with her – and of course it was about the whole baby thing. That was, after all, the most pressing issue at that moment. But it wasn't only about head circumferences or birthing positions; we also talked about our fears and worries and insights. I would have liked her even if we hadn't both had a huge belly.

Meena, it turned out, was an exception. That also became apparent during the PPCP course (the Prague Parent and Child Programme), a weekly meet-up for new parents and their babies. Six to eight grown-ups (mothers, invariably) sit on a mat in a warm room with their infants. The babies get undressed and you sing a song, a classic such as 'Wheels on the Bus'. Then you blow some bubbles and you talk. All in all, eight meetings, once a week, ninety minutes, for 125 smackers. Some enjoy it more than others. Meena and I were 'others'.

It didn't get any better when my son started nursery. The other parents had decided that the children were only allowed spelt biscuits without sugar, so the little ones wouldn't develop a taste 'for THAT'. There were regular discussions about which child was bullying which other and everything else that was going on – but mostly, what they didn't like. There was a WhatsApp group where we discussed why Lily had hit Laura and decided that Linus was always bossy. There were hours of conversations about the temperature in the building – too low or too high – which was revealing as to the ambient temperatures in the parents' households. I felt like I was the only person who was sending her child to nursery because I worked. The others seemed to have chosen the nursery as their new hobby.

A few weeks later I muted the WhatsApp group and only went through the hundreds of messages in the evening. When I read that Leonard had a headache again and scrolled through more than twenty good wishes and sad emojis from the other parents, it dawned on me: every time I have to read this drivel, I feel annoyed. In general, I'm happy to remain in blissful ignorance unless there's a major problem. The carers in the nursery have my full confidence, and I don't have to know who takes whose toys away. They give me ample information about my son and his behaviour, so I don't need 20 other parents' input. If there was anything I needed to know, they would tell me. My son meets his friends at various playgrounds in the afternoon; he will not suffer socially because of his difficult mother – so I decided not to give a damn about the other parents. I actually did it: I am probably the first human being to have left a nursery WhatsApp group.

At first it wasn't as liberating as I had anticipated, for the simple reason that if it was so easy to get them out of my life, presumably they had never really been in it. What I really *did* give a damn about was the other parents' opinions. Did they see me now as an antisocial loner? A misanthrope? But when I asked myself more precisely: was it really important to me what Lina's mum and Luca's dad thought of me, the answer was clear: no, not really. And then it happened. From deep within, a great feeling rose in me: 'Freedom!'

It's true. I am not exaggerating. It feels like *freedom*.

Listen closely to your gut feeling – and write down what you hear:

You will be leaving these WhatsApp groups:

....

You will delete the following contacts:

....

You will block these Facebook friends or groups:

....

Trying to understand childless friends

Before I had my baby, some people in my circle of friends became pregnant. And every time that happened, the respective parents disappeared without a trace once the baby was born.

Invites to dinner, for a drink or a coffee or anything else we had liked doing together before were cancelled. You try a few times, then think 'arseholes' and never try again.

When the day came that I pissed on the pregnancy stick and two lines appeared, it was immediately clear: I won't be like that. I would be a cool mama. I had saved up a few clever sayings in my head for this occasion:

'Children sleep when they are tired, no matter where.'

'When children are used to being in other people's houses, they sleep everywhere.'

'The main thing is that the children are included.'

'A change of scenery is good for children.'

For that reason, I wouldn't only be spending my days shopping (see above) and hanging around in cafés with my newborn baby, I also saw myself sitting in front of a tent at festivals, the baby in a sling, and when going on city trips I would have a cute little stroller for him. L. and I would have dinner together in our friends' large country kitchens, drinking a glass of wine while the baby was asleep in their bedroom next door. And on Fridays I would, of course, meet Anne for lunch in the Italian restaurant as usual, simply bringing my child with me. At every party I would be there, right at the centre – with my baby – and at some point, he would simply drop off to sleep on a sofa. The others would be impressed how easy my child was, and I would say: 'Children sleep when they are tired. We take ours everywhere, he is used to it.' And then there would be *oohs* and *aahs* all around because of our impressive child-rearing competence.

Ha ha.

Then the baby arrived.

After ten days of 'confinement' I decided it was time to turn into a cool mama, and we arranged to meet the in-laws in town. We were planning a little shopping trip. Mother-in-law could push the pram, and I had a chance to get out a bit. Everything was fine until we met up. From that moment on the baby cried.

I learned several things that day:

1. You somehow manage to get this new human being into the world and take it home, but you don't know how it functions.
2. Everyone around you, your partner included, assumes that you have some kind of innate, instinctive maternal knowledge.
3. After several minutes of crying other people stop looking on you in a kindly fashion and become rather resentful.

4. You must never forget nappies and baby wipes
   on any trip outside the house.

In the following weeks we got to know our son a bit better, knew what he liked (breasts, sleep in Mama's bed and having a bath) and what he didn't like (shopping, coffee shops and getting dressed), and we also learned that he liked a certain routine. All the wisdom and insights after that could be reduced to the following fact:

As long as the baby is allowed to follow its own routines, everything goes smoothly. If that is not possible, it's shit. That is a situation you cannot really communicate to childless friends:

'I know that Libby is coming, but we really have to go now ...'

'Why? The baby is completely relaxed.'

'Yes, that's why we are going now, before he has a meltdown, which will happen in exactly half an hour.'

You can feel it viscerally how your loved ones are inwardly shaking their heads. Until they have a baby too.

I don't go for lunch with Anne on Fridays any more because at one o'clock, at the latest, he needs his nap. In his cot. If we are somewhere else, he wakes up or doesn't drop off with excitement, and then the whole afternoon will be hell. No matter how often I went, with best intentions, to a restaurant, café or party – it didn't work. Simply because you are meant to be enjoying these activities with the other people present, but instead you are permanently (or very frequently) busy with the child. The chance to have a halfway decent conversation over a coffee tends to be zero. The planned dinners with friends, however, went all right, as long as:

- We arrived early enough that the baby dropped off at some point, despite the excitement.
- He couldn't turn himself around and fall off the bed. (When that happened, we asked whether we could make up a little bed on the floor – and there it was again: the inward shaking of the head ...)
- We resigned ourselves to waking him up a few hours later to take him home in the car and to cope with the lack of sleep the next day
- L. and I could manage to keep our eyes open after half past nine.

Surprise, surprise, we didn't go to many dinner parties. In fact we didn't go to many other events that required us to be awake after half past nine.

This is very difficult to communicate to childless couples. There is a reason they've invented these life-size baby dolls for teenagers. They cry and need attention and demonstrate to the youngsters what it means to have a baby. I have contemplated buying such a doll so that I give it to anyone who says why don't I come to the party and L. can look after the baby, and tell them to look after the thing for a few days. But they cost a thousand pounds.

It is also difficult to communicate that you like spending time with your baby. I want to be with him, even though the child's attractions are not that obvious to outsiders. It is also very difficult to explain that the few things we do in our free time are dependent on whether there is a lot of space for running around, whether there are other children and whether there is a cushioned floor – rather than the quality of the cocktails.

A lot changed when our son got older. By now he can get out of bed and leave the friend's bedroom on his own. He can grab everything that is sharp, pointed or precious. He can leave a beer garden unobserved and run into the street, he can strangle himself with his scarf, fall and hit his head. Again, we are extremely distracted when meeting up with other people, but less by the baby's crying than by our attempts to keep our offspring alive. 'But it's great being a parent!' we assure our childless friends, who exchange meaningful glances.

This seeming contradiction – it cannot be explained rationally. At some point I had to concede: I am not a cool mama. Not cool in the sense that childless people imagine a cool mama to be. I can't explain to our friends why that is so. My explanations sound like justifications, so everybody thinks we have gone completely gaga. That is why I don't even try any more. Trying to ensure the understanding of childless couples – forget it.

What I offer now is only facts that can either be accepted by childless people or rejected. They will not be discussed any more.

'There is a cool party next Saturday? Great! We are not going.'

'Brunch at Charlie's tomorrow at one? Have a good time!'

'Go for a coffee? OK, maybe between ten and eleven?'

Cinema, football or someone's poetry slam I can dismiss without batting an eyelid. Just like that. These days I have a standard reply to this kind of suggestion: *We will probably not come, but we love you anyway.*

There are friends, though, even some without children, who I can do things with despite the baby. These meet-ups are lovely, and they are wonderful people, because they sense instinctively what is possible and what is not. They are not disappointed or put out when a plan is cancelled at the last minute because of tummy aches, teething or I DON'T KNOW WHAT IS WRONG.

As an alternative, I ask people to come for breakfast. At about seven in the morning. We are always fighting fit at that time.

And I also want everybody to know: *Don't give up on us – we will be back, when the conditions are right.*

6

Love

- Guessing
- Understanding
- Everybody else
- Love yourself
- Shared hobbies
- Your partner's faults

Most people have some experience of ruthlessness where love is involved. Either they have dished it out themselves, or, perhaps, they have encountered someone else with that attitude. Most of us will have played on both sides at some point in our lives, and, of course, one is definitely better than the other.

There are years when you become so ruthless in relationships that people just come and go in droves. I will not bore you with some excellent examples of this from my life, maybe due to some exes of mine who might take offence if they read about it.

At some point, however, when things are running pretty smoothly, you'll find someone who is not completely bananas, whom you want to keep, and then it gets really complicated.

For twelve years now, L. and I have had a so-called 'life partnership', and I like him just as much now as I did at the beginning. Even though I could sometimes strangle him. He is my Mr Right, the One and Only, the knight without shining armour. But I never knew before that even happy-ever-after princes throw their socks on the bedroom floor. That is the one big mystery: love and relationships are the most important part of our lives, but nobody teaches you how to do it. You need to find out everything yourself. I ask myself whether it would make sense to swap a few lessons in school, maybe the ones about the wriggling dance of the honeybee, for some enlightened information about love. At least the basics:

- Princes and princesses are only human.
- Being 'in love' doesn't last and that is normal.
- It's also normal to want to throw your partner off the balcony.
- The sex slows down.
- How to argue without being nasty.

- And all the other things you shouldn't give a toss about.

Guessing

This is a classic one. I don't know how much time in my life I have wasted with second-guessing and interpreting the behaviour, words and reactions of L. Here is a single example – and it's true:

One day we had arranged to meet for dinner in a lovely little restaurant (it was before the baby arrived; we actually went out for dinner then). That evening L. was kind of peculiar from the start. At first I thought it was because I had been a bit late, but he didn't say anything. He didn't speak very much at all, and the mood stayed somewhat flat throughout the meal.

'Come on,' I said and took his hand. 'Let's go somewhere for a nightcap.' I hoped he would tell me what the matter was. He agreed, but in the bar (it was before the baby; we went to bars then) he still hardly said anything and just fiddled with the straw in his cocktail. So I asked him: 'What's the matter?'

And he said: 'Nothing.'

'Are you mad at me? Have I said or done something stupid?' I prodded, but his reaction was non-committal.

'No, I'm not mad at you,' he said, but he remained detached and his forehead stayed wrinkled.

When we drove home, I tousled his hair and said: 'I love you,' and then he smiled and pressed my hand briefly and drove on. I still didn't have a clue what was going on, and the fact he hadn't reciprocated my 'I love you' shook me a bit. It was as if there was a huge wall between us, and I didn't even know why!

At home, he didn't pay any attention to me and switched the computer on, while I loaded the dishwasher in the kitchen. My heart was aching, and I thought: is it the end? Was there another woman? Did he have to check the computer so late because of that? When would he tell me? Eventually I went to bed, and L., completely distant, didn't even look up. When he came to bed later, he stayed on his side to avoid touching me, and when I pushed my foot alongside his, he withdrew. That made me cry. Whatever he was thinking, he wasn't thinking of me, but presumably another woman. So I cried, while L. snored.

The next day I only saw L. again in the evening, and he said, as soon as he came in, that he needed to talk with me. *'This is it,'* I thought and sat down at the kitchen table, ready for everything. Would he want to move out? *Does he want me to move out?* I was thinking as he looked me in the eyes.

'Alex, I have tried, but I don't know how to go on,' he said, and I felt the tears coming. 'I have eliminated all possible reasons, but it still makes this funny noise. I think it is the gearbox.'

We stared at each other for a few seconds. Then we said at the same time:

Me: 'What?'

Him: 'Are you crying?'

These things happen. Our damned, fucking shit car was broken. That was all. L. was speechless when I explained to him that I had thought he wanted to end the relationship. He actually got a bit angry. I know that because he said: 'I think I might be a little bit angry!' Then we blamed everything on my lively imagination, embraced each other and promised various things: I would not second-guess bullshit any more and take it for the truth, and L. would talk a bit more.

I always remember this story when I notice that I am second-guessing something, mentally speculating why someone is doing this or that and what could be the reason. It is normal to be suspicious and to assume dangers where there aren't any. It has been useful for human evolution. But we no longer live in palaeolithic times, sabre-tooth tigers and all. You should just ask when you want to know something, and, of course, you must try to believe the answers.

Men very often say exactly what they are thinking. Soon after the shit car story, L. said: 'I like your friend Jana.' I briefly thought that this must mean he would do anything to go to bed with Jana, to marry her and have children with her, while I grew old and lonely and got invited for dinner by them every now and then.

It is very liberating not to torture yourself with such nonsense any more but instead to simply take what the other person says at face value, which is how it's meant to be taken.

When was the last time you did some really bad second-guessing?

Here's a little table of definitions what your partner might mean when he says something:

SAYS	MEANS
Nothing	Nothing
X is nice	X is nice
I am tired	I am tired
Great!	Really great

Understanding

'I don't understand' as a reaction to something somebody says or does very often means: 'I think this is totally stupid.' But you really want to understand the person you love. At first, we want to know everything – 'I want to know *everything* about you!' – and then we want to *understand* everything. But as soon as the other person says they want to know *everything* it dawns on us: *No, he/she doesn't.* The same applies to understanding: *No, he/she is not able to.* It doesn't work the other way around either. Sometimes we don't understand anything.

There are many things I don't understand about L. For example, I don't understand why he doesn't ring his best friend Sion more often.

Men and their friends are strange. When Sion and L. meet, they don't seem to do anything together. And they only meet up twice a year. They don't email in between or ring or Skype. When I ask L. how Sion is, whether he is happy in his relationship and whether he likes his job, whether his parents are still alive, L. looks at me as if I have lost the plot. He has internalised the main rule of male friendships: *As long as your friend doesn't say anything to the contrary, everything is OK.*

L. only gets worried when Sion actually rings. Then something has happened. If he announces a visit outside their normal schedule, L. puts beer in the fridge, because something really bad must have happened. Not that they then discuss the problem all night – no. Sion explains the situation, and then they get drunk, and sometimes one of them sighs. As I said, I don't get it.

I don't understand either that L. runs forty-two kilometres in one go! On foot. When we met, he was preparing for a marathon. For me, up to that point, a marathon was just one of those stupid events when all the important streets in the city are closed.

But when L. told me about the fantastic atmosphere and how good you feel when you have actually finished it, I watched one and came to the conclusion that it is simply one of those stupid events when some strategically important streets in the city centre get closed. Seriously: I do not understand the fun of things you only enjoy when they are over. I'd rather not do it and I am very happy that I don't have to run forty-two kilometres.

Another thing I find hard to get is L.'s friendship with Dennis, a complete idiot. We share a mutual and deep dislike of each other. Or that L. likes fishing – have you ever seen how they get the hook out of the poor fish's lip? You instinctively touch your lower lip and wince.

L., however, shakes his head in disbelief when he notices that I spend hours looking for a lovely house for us online. 'But we will never be able to afford a house,' he says. He doesn't understand my answer: 'I am not buying, I am only looking.'

Whether they breed orchids or go to tribute band concerts: there are a lot of things we will never quite understand about our loved ones. Aside from the not-so-nice things, like the fishing hook, it's likely that they will also have some really stupid characteristics, such as L.'s strategy of problem solving. That actually drives me close to a nervous breakdown. He simply puts his head in the sand and hopes the problem will solve itself. Do I understand it? Not at all! It gets on my nerves, it concerns me, and I could pull his head off when he is like that. Can I change it? Unfortunately – no, and I really do like L. But I don't have to understand everything. I can accept that he is not perfect, as I am probably not perfect either. If it comes to it, I can even listen when he comes back from fishing and tells me about the ones he very nearly got, and I can love how he looks when he tells me.

Loving oneself

You probably know the saying: 'You can only really love someone else if you love yourself.' This sentence has, in one way or another, managed to obtain the status of 'great wisdom'. Whenever I read it, a cute picture postcard pops up in my head of a cute sunset with the sentence in cute lettering printed on it.

It is an utterly stupid sentence.

If it were really true, a large part of mankind would be unable to love, because most people have problems with loving themselves and with their self-esteem. Some people have phases when they don't like themselves very much, others only hate themselves in front of a mirror in changing rooms, others again are constantly critical of themselves, and others would like to be someone else altogether. And then there are those people who think they are utter shit. In short: none of us is a perfect ten. Despite this, the false belief persists that if we could just learn to feel good about ourselves then our love life would magically work out. As if you could work out something like love. It's not maths. Until then, we remain second-class and can only attract second- and third-class partners, and quite a few exes seem to confirm the theory. Whole armies of people run to therapists and workshops to 'improve' themselves in the hope that they, finally, will be able to have a happy relationship with a Class A person. There it is, the sunset.

Thank God, the fact is that it is perfectly possible to love somebody even if you are not a sparkling example of humankind. You can carry the burden of your childhood trauma and still love someone. Otherwise, the world would be a very lonely place.

If all you can say about yourself is that you are somehow OK, at least not worse than others – that is good enough. And if you can say that about your lover, then nothing – NOTHING – can prevent you from being very happy.

All other people

Once you have settled down with your partner, you can take stock after you've been together a while. Do you still think your loved one is great? Brilliant! Do you find him or her impossible every now and then? Yes? That is completely normal. Look at the ratio between 'great' and 'impossible'. Are there more 'great' moments than 'impossible'? Congratulations. You have made a good choice.

Before I met L., the ratio between 'great' and 'impossible' with previous boyfriends always shifted towards the latter, until only 'impossible' moments remained. Sometimes it went slowly, at other times very quickly, and before you knew it you had to go to the hairdresser again, paint your flat or whatever was necessary to keep you from drowning in a flood of tears. Since L. has been a part of my life I have tried to follow the advice of a well-known author who compares finding a partner with going to a restaurant. You look at the menu, get an overview of what is on offer, and then choose the item you like. Done. Then you give the menu back and stop thinking about what else you could have chosen and what you might be missing.[8]

As soon as I had given the menu back, everything became easier. There is a lot less stress when you close the chapter of looking for a partner. He is the one, I told myself, congratulated him and me, and to this day, this hasn't changed. It helps that the men I meet are nice enough to have a drink with, but are nothing compared with L. It's quite wonderful to know this, believe me. Even if George Clooney (not the Clooney Clone) turned up in the Pimpernel tomorrow, I am sure he would never be as funny as L. when we got married. He did *Monty Python*'s 'Ministry of Silly Walks' with me. And have you ever seen Clooney before he had his teeth done? Well ...

Looking for a partner is a bit like looking at the jam and marmalade shelves in the supermarket. You simply

---

8 E.v.Hirschhausen, *Glück kommt selten allein*. ISBN 978-3499624841

want a nice raspberry jam, but it gets complicated. Will you take the one with the organic label or the one with the bits in? That one has a pretty label but isn't organic, and there is the branded stuff and the very cheap stuff, but the packaging is awful. This can go on for quite a while. You invest a lot of time studying and analysing it, and in the end, you take the chosen jam jar home, and it still only tastes of – guess what – raspberry jam. OK, in that case you hardly ever ponder what would have happened if you had made a different choice, but exactly that happens in our real love lives all the time. At some point you pick up the dirty socks for a hundredth time that your lover ALWAYS THROWS DIRECTLY NEXT TO THE LAUNDRY BASKET, you remember last night when, again, he fell asleep, mouth wide open, in front of the telly, and then you start musing about how he's put on weight in the last few weeks ... And then at the same moment, a song comes on the radio that reminds you of HIM. Which HIM? Don't pretend, there is only one HIM. Don't fall into the trap. Just stop worrying.

Shared hobbies

Shared hobbies are brilliant, aren't they? When together you, arm in arm ... well?

The only thing L. and I have always enjoyed doing together is walking. Partly because of the dog, as he likes it as well. Apart from that, shared hobbies are difficult, if you don't have any. I always had the feeling we should have something in common, something we both liked doing. If you have a lot of fun with other people going riding, doing amateur dramatics or going to pottery lessons – how amazing would it be with your lover? I have really tried. Even fantasy role-playing games, to please an ex. But I had imagined I would be dressing up and running through woods and doing magic. Not at all. The role-play game I took part in involved a few pale guys sitting around a table playing dice and then looking at two large books to find out where to put the pieces next and what it would mean. In hindsight, I had wasted my time contemplating long and hard what to wear. In fact, looking back, I think it was the most boring hour of my whole life. Jana would swear that there is nothing more boring than a hobby of one of her exes who spent hours doing 3-D jigsaws. Despite her reservations, she worked with him on a 3-D model of King Ludwig's Castle for hours, always in the hope that this highly original but sad pastime would just be a phase (it wasn't).

The things one does for love ...

L. must have thought this when, because of me, he sat on a horse for the first time in his life. I was absolutely sure that once he tried it out, he would understand. As it was so important to me (and maybe because I put a bit of pressure on him), one fine Sunday morning he gave it a try. I had organised the horse and the teacher, the sun was shining, everything was perfect. I saw us galloping through the landscape; we could live in the country and keep our own horses, maybe breed them ... By the time the lesson was over, I had dreamt up a little life plan in which I would look after the foals and L. would mend our white picket fences. L., however, the very moment the lesson was over, informed me that he would never ever get on a horse again. He had hurt his balls so much that for a week he had to do his work in the office standing up. Why would anyone be content with one horsepower, he argued, when there were so many options with much more horsepower that you could reliably operate with just a few levers and buttons and pedals? And why did he have to push his heels downwards on the stirrups all the time – there wasn't even a pedal there! It seemed clear that the path towards our horse-breeding farm would be bumpy.

To get his own back, L. asked me to do some sport with him. Running I declined politely, but L. goes swimming, too, and maybe I would like that? Not so many foals in that picture, but OK.

So, I accompanied L. to the swimming pool, bathing hat and all in the bag. There was a nice familiar scent of chlorine and an echo that I remembered from last time I went to the pool... when I was twelve. L. got going straight away, and from then on, I could only see one half of his face, left-right, alternately. And his arms. The only women I could see did the same, and they were all wearing dark one-piece suits. Only one wasn't wearing goggles and was sporting a green and red bikini with a jungle pattern on. *Moi*!

I did try. I swam this way and then that way and again, this way and that way and again ... and nearly drowned with boredom. There are no visual distractions in swimming pools. When you go walking, the landscape changes, but swimming is like walking in a completely bare hall and then you have to turn around after a hundred metres.

After that experience I sat down in the jacuzzi to bubble away my cellulite. Then I went to the sauna to give my hair mask time to work. That was quite pleasant but wasn't much like a shared hobby.

'But we have to do something together,' I wailed in the car on the way home while we were stopped at a traffic light.

L. replied: 'Do you mean like those people over there?' and nodded out of the window on my side. There was a group of bikers on their highly polished machines, clad in the usual leather. Staring at the ladies who were all on the back seats, it dawned on me: I have been in that position. With H., L.'s predecessor, because I had thought we needed an activity to share, for God's sake. And before I knew it, I was sitting, like my predecessor, on the pillion behind H. every weekend, sweating in the summer months, freezing in winter, and going with him to 'meetings'. At those meetings we would stand around a bike in small groups and discuss the suspension struts and which MOT garage had okayed this monstrous exhaust. I was nearly tempted to go back to fantasy role-play. Then some nutter would push the back wheel while applying the handbrake until the tyre burst and the tarmac was rubberised, and then we all went home. I could have spent so many lovely weekends at home on the sofa, binge-watching a new series. Maybe I could have even learned something important, such as sign language. As if confirming this, the lights changed and all the ladies tapped the helmet of the man in front of them to start driving, and I felt a tap inside my head as well.

I will never again spend a single minute of my holy free time on some hobby that I do not like or care about. Furthermore, I will never again waste a single minute of my precious free time thinking about having a shared hobby.

Forget it.

Partner's faults

Oh God, I can hardly bear to think about some of my previous boyfriends. I always thought it was only me who went out with those idiots. When they said on the radio they had discovered a large number of duds in town, I thought of my exes and nodded ... but it turned out they meant bombs. Surprisingly, a lot of other women I know had the same thought.

After a brief survey among my women friends I can now profile some stereotypes most of us have met at some point in time:

- The long-haired, slim type who plays guitar, can draw well or writes short stories and tends to have mood swings – sometimes combined with the skills *rock climbing* or *surfing*. A dream of a man. When he is in love with you, he writes songs for you and you become the heroine of his stories. Only rational things such as clothes, furniture, jobs, money or cleaning are alien concepts for him.
- The sporty type with well-trained muscles and dragon or tribal tattoos, who will carry you into the bedroom, but is not very useful outside it.
- The rather pale type with the sensitive skin whose sense of adventure is satisfied when he dreams of building a pond in his own garden and who to this day talks of the bungee jump four years ago that he very nearly did.
- The self-important smartypants who doesn't only get free entrance to the clubs but also greets the bouncers with a handshake. He knows such-and-such a celeb personally, but you have to google their name.
- The beau with the flawless skin and the very white teeth. His background is posh,

and only the best will do for him. He goes snowboarding, water skiing and Papa has given him an expensive car. He is the type you would introduce to your mother, because she can boast about him at the next family party.

In some cases, and when the guys get a bit older, some of these quirks become less pronounced or are lost completely. The long-haired surfer opens a shop and even gets to grips with the paperwork. The handshake-smartypants finds his pomposity a bit embarrassing in hindsight. It all happens. One lives, and one learns. And the ladies, too, learn and one day they get to the point when they have sussed it. You can't have everything. Maybe stick with an old wisdom:

1. Attractive
2. Funny
3. Emotionally stable

Choose two of them.

With this insight, have a look at the best available types on offer, make a choice and try to adjust things where they are not satisfactory. Though that is itself a stressful process. Whole armies of women have despaired when trying to change their men or their habits, or as we might call it: to 'optimise' them. Surface changes are quite easy. Clothes, hairstyles, beards and a few pounds too many – that is all doable. The awkward habits are rather more persistent.

I nearly get into crisis mode every time I pick up L.'s socks from the bedroom floor. It may sound trivial, but I have been doing it for years, and for years I have nagged him about it. Jana doesn't think it a problem at all, but she gets mad every time her lover comes back from shopping. He always buys the wrong bread, or the jam Jana doesn't like, or the yoghurt with the bits in, or sour apples rather than sweet ones. Jana's anger rises the moment the poor chap comes home with the shopping bag. Is that silly? Maybe. I find it a bit over the top, too, but there is always something. Maybe your partner has an annoying habit of cracking his knuckles, or he leaves lots of stubble in the washbasin after shaving, or he always checks ten times whether he has locked the car, leaves his dirty plates on the table, cuts his toenails in the living room, is never on time, always forgets two out of three things from the shops or you simply want to kill him when he snores.

There are habits that can generally be stopped (though just to put a damper on things: not the snoring). When I met L., whenever he sat down to a meal he would say, 'Yummy yummy!' At home, in restaurants, when he accompanied me to a gala dinner and even when the French ambassador plus his entourage was sitting at our table.

I would get nervous the moment he pulled back the chair to sit down. Would he say it? Or not? If he saw my threatening glances, would he pull himself together? But he would be kind of absent-minded: 'Yummy yummy!' It drove me crazy. Once when we went for a meal around the corner from us, the pizza was just being served and L. opened his mouth. 'Y...' He didn't get any further.

'DON'T SAY IT!' I hissed, and the guests on nearby tables, plus the waiter bringing our calzone, looked at me as if *I* was completely off my trolley. L. smiled a little satisfied smile, and I hated him for the rest of the evening. I eventually managed to stop him making this silly remark. It took time, and it made me look stupid on occasion, but it worked in the end.

What doesn't work at all is the thing with the socks. I get angry and pick them up. It's not an option to simply leave them, like Anne had recommended; there would just be more and more of them.

Why I get so annoyed about the bleeding socks and Jana about the wrong bread has to do with the fact that you infer a certain attitude from their behaviour. I assume that L. thinks: *'The idiot, she will tidy them up,'* and Jana hears: *'He doesn't care about me, otherwise he would know what I like.'*

The funny thing is that I can remember arguments with my mother when I was a teenager: I would always spread my clothes all over the floor in my bedroom, and she would get really upset and say something like: 'You probably think that stupid me will tidy up after you.' But I can also remember very clearly that I never had any thoughts at all when doing it. I never thought about my mother in the slightest when I threw my things on the floor.

And L. doesn't either. I also know that Jana's boyfriend loves her to bits and would do anything for her – the thing with the bread is the only thing he doesn't get quite right.

All in all, I have come to realise that it is over ten years now that I have been getting angry about socks. Can you believe it? Socks! Ten years! That really is a lot of anger, when you look at it like that. But if I hadn't gotten angry about the socks a decade ago, the situation would be exactly the same. I would still be picking them up and throwing them in the laundry basket. I could have saved myself a lot of anger, because now I have the insight of the century: *If you are not annoyed – you are not annoyed.*

Buddha would probably have expressed it a bit better:

To cling on to your anger is like holding a
hot piece of coal in your hand in order to throw
it at someone.

So there you have it: my decision not to get annoyed any more about trivial things – but it doesn't always work. I still get annoyed, because sometimes I simply can't help it. What does help is the following insight.

L., in terms of dirty socks, has a kind of limited vision. His vision regarding footwear is so limited that it doesn't trigger any reaction in him. Presumably this optical disability has to do with the well-known syndrome of Ground-Blindness, which makes it very difficult to recognise textiles lying on the floor.

And Jana's boyfriend suffers from a Particular Preference Amnesia. His memory regarding Jana's food preferences is limited. It is so much easier to say: '*He simply can't do it; it's an illness*', than to get annoyed day after day about the shopping or the fucking socks. Don't give a toss. On the other hand, I am glad that L. now recognises my passion for lovely shoes as a Dependency on Podiatric Objects Syndrome.

If, of course, your darling suddenly discovers a penchant for blonde women in their twenties, it might be difficult to diagnose it as an infectious disease caused by Lightly Pigmented Female-philia and not to get annoyed. Quite the opposite. Maybe in that case it might be an idea to reject this particular loved one. But when it is about everyday things and your beloved has been a good choice in many other ways, then my advice would be to simply not give a damn about it.

Here's a table of some of the most common syndromes and how to recognise them:

What does he do?	What do I assume?	What is it really?
He uses the last of the toilet paper and doesn't get a new roll out	He doesn't care if I'm stuck without toilet paper	Partial short-term memory loss
He forgets birthdays, anniversaries, etc.	He just doesn't care	Doesn't have much of a long-term memory either
He never puts the top back on the toothpaste	He thinks I'm a cleaner	Serious toothpaste-top-phobia
He doesn't listen	He doesn't care about what I have to say	Limited auditive capacity
He snores	He doesn't care whether I can sleep or not	Blockage of the airways

Here is your personal table of quirks for your loved one. Please add the appropriate medical condition for the phenomenon and then... *whoosh*, don't give a damn!

What do they do?	What do I assume?	What is it really?

And Finally

I guess I have annoyed you on several occasions while you were reading this book.

Maybe I have offended you by dissing your favourite music, or I have bitched about your favourite sport, or you are my boss ('Hi, Brian!'), or I have otherwise put my foot in it. Whatever it is or was, please do give a toss about the book, because I didn't mean to annoy you. I just wanted to give you some examples from my life of how wonderful it can be when you cut out what makes you unhappy, and learn how to be a bit of a dick. Naturally, in my life these will be different from the things in your life. But I hope you feel like you can now say what you want, ask for what you need and get the life you deserve. GO AHEAD and be a dick. Nobody can stop you.

I wish you luck!